The Hiker's Guide
to ALBERTA

by
Will Harmon

FALCON™

Falcon Press® Publishing Co., Inc.
Helena, Montana

Falcon Press Publishing Co., Inc.
P.O. Box 1718, Helena, MT 59624

All text, maps, and photos by the author except as noted.
Cover Photo: by Will Harmon of Mount Andromeda

Library of Congress Cataloging-in-Publication Data

Harmon, Will.
    The hiker's guide to Alberta / Will Harmon
        p.   cm.
    Originally published : c1992.
    ISBN 1-56044-370-7
        1. Hiking--Alberta--Guidebooks.   2. Alberta--Description and
    travel--Guidebooks.   I. Title.
GV199.44.C22A424   1994   91-77719
796.5'2'097123--dc20   CIP

CAUTION

Outdoor recreation activities are by their very nature potentially
hazardous. All participants in such activities must assume the responsi-
bility for their own actions and safety. The information contained in this
guidebook cannot replace sound judgment and good decision making
skills, which help reduce risk exposure, nor does the scope of this book
allow for disclosure of all the potential hazards and risks involved in
such activities.

Learn as much as possible about the outdoor recreation activities you
participate in, prepare for the unexpected, and be safe and cautious.
The reward will be a safer and more enjoyable experience.

 Text pages printed on recycled paper.

ACKNOWLEDGMENTS

Writing a book is the surest way to meet new friends and estrange one's family. That I have done the first without suffering the second is a tribute to the many people who responded so warmly to questions, letters, and phone calls, and to the saintly patience of Rose, Evan, and Benjamin.

A special thanks goes to the authors who contributed hike descriptions: Peter Allen, Keith Bocking, Carter Cox, Kerry Hope, Natalie Humenuk-Bourke, Lorraine Robinson, and Randy Roch. Look for their bylines at the end of the descriptions.

Others helped ease the hardships of the trail and gave generously of their experience and expertise, recommending trails, poring over maps, and discussing the local flora and fauna. Thanks go to Peter Achuff, Mac Bates, Dan Linton, Doug Loneman, John Nesbitt, Andre Savaria, Nancy Smith, David A. Vetra, and Ed Whitelock.

CONTENTS

LOCATION OF HIKES

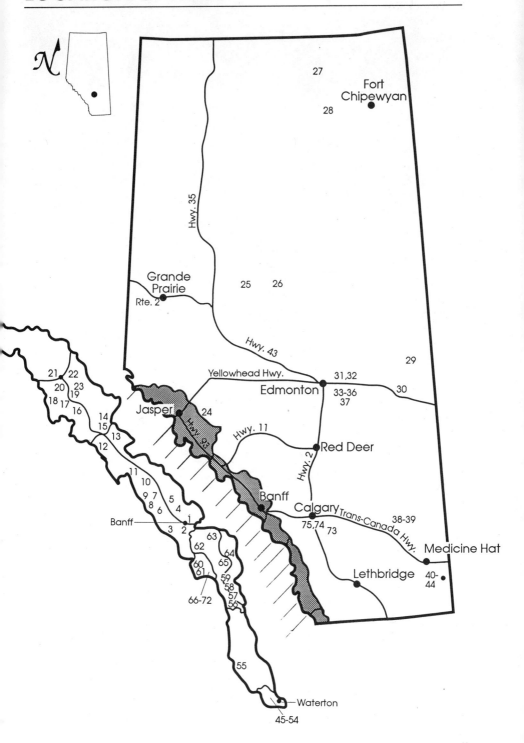

Lower Consolation Lake, with Bident Mountain in the background.

HIKING IN ALBERTA, AN INTRODUCTION

Alberta's landscape is more diverse than perhaps any other Canadian province, from arid badlands and rolling prairie to lake-studded aspen parkland, vast boreal forest, and endless ranges of ice-clad mountains. Here the four compass points meet: the eastern prairie collides with the western mountains and the great plains sweep up from the south to blend with the northern forest.

For the hiker, such a landscape offers a bewildering array of hiking terrain—the spruce-shaded coulees of Cypress Hills and the scorched moonscape of Dinosaur Provincial Park, the beaver ponds and balsam poplars of the Cooking Lake Hills and the windswept timberline of Jasper's jagged peaks, a heron rookery within Calgary's city limits and the grazing grounds of wood bison on the Peace River delta. Each area invites exploration, each trail caters to our different moods, dispositions, and abilities.

The Hiker's Guide to Alberta highlights seventy-five of the best hikes throughout the province, describing in detail over 800 kilometres of trail. Included here are world renowned routes through the spectacular scenery of the Canadian Rockies as well as less celebrated trails within the many far-flung provincial parks. Through text, maps, and photos, the book accurately portrays each hike's character, location, degree of difficulty, and special attractions.

Of course, there are hundreds, perhaps thousands, of other trails across Alberta left unmentioned here. Use these seventy-five hikes as a starting point, an introduction to the hiking opportunities to be uncovered in each corner of the province.

Weather

In the western mountains

Alberta's backbone of mountain ranges catches more precipitation than any other part of the province, most of it coming as snow during the winter months. The hiking season runs from July through October, although some lower elevation trails may be open by mid-May in some years depending on snowpack. Avoid hiking on saturated trails; it is muddy, unrewarding work and hard on the soil and vegetation. Trails are often wet in May and June, and snowfields linger through July on many alpine trails. In the mountains, snow, rain, and brilliant sunshine can occur on any day of the year, sometimes all within a single hour, and wind is an almost constant factor particularly at higher elevations. Days can be hot during the summer, but nights are always cool. Snowstorms are likely in September, along with plummeting temperatures, and by late October many ridge trails and high passes are impassable. When travelling in the mountains, be prepared for extreme weather and always carry a raincoat or water resistant windshell.

Be prepared for sudden weather changes in the mountains. Raingear is a must.

On the prairie

Alberta's prairie rolls from the foothills east to Saskatchewan and from Highway 9 south to the United States border. Most of this region falls under the rainshadow of the mountains to the west but still receives more moisture than the southern expanse of the Great Plains in the United States. The hiking season is longer here than elsewhere in the province, extending from April through November in some years. Spring often brings steady rain for two to three days at a time, while brief but intense thunderstorms are more the rule in June, July, and August. Rains quickly turn most prairie trails (and dirt roads) to gumbo, a slippery, boot-sucking mud that is neither land nor water. Summer days are usually dry and can be extremely hot—the well-prepared hiker will carry plenty of drinking water. By September the bugs are gone and trails are at their best, but the weather is less predictable and north winds may bring a rush of arctic air. In dry years, good hiking weather lingers into October and a scattering of days in November.

In the northern forests

Nearly two-thirds of Alberta is covered by boreal forest and aspen parkland. The hiking season here generally begins in June and lasts through October, though some trails may be closed by high water into early summer due to heavy rains or seasonal flooding. Daily temperatures range from hot to comfortably cool through spring and summer, and fall comes early to the northern regions. The sheer number of bogs and lakes through much of this country, and the dense woodlands, lend a higher humidity to the air, and morning and evening fogs are not uncommon. Insect populations thrive with so much standing water, and from June through August the hordes of mosquitoes and flies are so pervasive they seem to be an atmospheric phenomenon like rain or wind—a windy day is a godsend.

MAP LEGEND

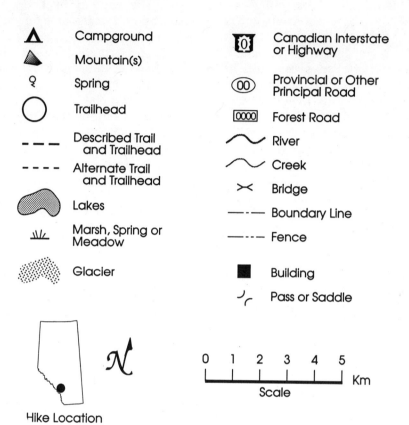

△	Campground	🄌	Canadian Interstate or Highway
◤	Mountain(s)		
☿	Spring	⬭00⬭	Provincial or Other Principal Road
◯	Trailhead	▢0000▢	Forest Road
– – –	Described Trail and Trailhead	〰	River
- - - -	Alternate Trail and Trailhead	⌒	Creek
▰	Lakes	✕	Bridge
⟋⟍	Marsh, Spring or Meadow	—·—	Boundary Line
⟒⟒⟒	Glacier	—··—	Fence
		▮	Building
		⌐ᵣ	Pass or Saddle

Hike Location

```
0   1   2   3   4   5
|___|___|___|___|___|  Km
        Scale
```

Maps

Most of the hikes described here can be negotiated without a map. But even veteran hikers often carry maps with them to help identify landmarks and alternative hiking routes along the way. The maps in this book are intended as basic representations of the trails and major features for each hike.

For more detailed information, refer to the topographic maps in the National Park Series and the 1:50,000 scale maps in the National Topographic Series. The Banff National Park sheet (which includes Kootenay and Yoho national parks in British Columbia) and the Jasper National Park sheet are scaled at 1:200,000, while the Waterton Lakes National Park map is 1:50,000. All three show sufficient detail for hiking and can be purchased from sporting goods stores, book stores, and park visitor centres in townsites in and near the parks. Other maps in the 1:50,000 series can be purchased from authorized dealers throughout the province and from the Maps Alberta office, Land Information Services Division, 2nd Floor, North Tower, Petroleum Plaza, 9945 - 108 Street, Edmonton, Alberta, Canada, T5K 2G6, phone: (403) 427-3520. For a complete list of available maps, write for the handy Maps Alberta catalogue at the above address.

Many of the provincial parks also provide maps and interpretive brochures of hiking trails within their borders. These brochures can be requested from the park staff by writing to the provincial park address given with each hike description.

The Hiker's Ethic

Hiking is an act of freedom, a measure of one's independence from the

Alberta's backcountry promises unspoiled scenery and solitude.
Randy Roch photo

civilised world. But civilisation is portable, and too many of us bring its ugly side with us: candy wrappers on the trail, trampled lakeshores and alpine summits, beer cans in the fire pit, squirrels and grey jays begging for the next handout, axe-bitten trees. As the number of hikers increases, the damage grows more severe. If the wilderness experience is to be preserved for everyone, each of us must follow a simple ethic—tread the land gently, respect its inhabitants, and be courteous to fellow hikers. Here are a few specific suggestions.

Don't litter. Even the smallest scrap of tissue, foil, or orange peel blights the landscape, serving as an unwanted reminder of city life to the next hiker. If you pack it in, pack it out.

Stay on trails, particularly in boggy areas or when trekking above timberline. If you must cross untracked alpine meadows, spread out rather than travelling single file. Also, do not cut switchbacks. Such shortcuts channel rain and snowmelt, scarring the hillside and eroding the trail.

Consider wearing running shoes or boots with less rugged soles. These disrupt the soil less and are gentler on plant life underfoot.

Don't pick flowers or unduly disturb rocks and soil. Leave antlers, arrowheads, and other potential souvenirs where you find them so the next hiker can enjoy them in a natural setting.

Don't feed or approach wildlife. Feeding animals, even squirrels and small birds, disrupts their normal food-gathering habits. Animals that become reliant on handouts may not prepare adequately for winter and often become nuisances to other hikers, raiding tents and backpacks and sometimes clawing or biting the outstretched hand. In most parks, feeding or enticing wildlife is illegal.

When in the backcountry, use a gas cookstove instead of a fire. Cookstoves are quicker to light and heat food more efficiently. Fires are prohibited in many areas because of a scarcity of wood or the risk of wildfire. Building campfires depletes the forest of logs and other dead wood, an important niche for insects, small mammals, and birds, and a vital source of nutrients that replenish the soil. Also do not cut live trees. In emergencies, when a fire is needed for warmth or drying gear, use an established fire ring. If none is available, cut and lift a small circle of topsoil and build a small fire of sticks on the mineral soil. When the fire is out, scatter the cold ashes widely and replace the topsoil.

Wash dishes and bathe at least fifty metres away from streams and lakes. Use biodegradable soap and use it sparingly. Keep a clean camp and always hang your food—even during the day if you're away from camp—to protect it from bears and other animals. Put all cookware and clothes worn while cooking in a food bag or pack and hang it between two trees at least four metres from the ground and one metre from either tree. If possible, hang food 300 metres or more from camp. Many of Alberta's parks provide steel cables for hanging food at backcountry campsites.

Bury all human waste and tissue paper. Dig a shallow pit (about fifteen to twenty centimetres deep) in well-drained soil at least 100 metres from all surface water. When group camping, use small individual pits rather than a common latrine.

In addition to treating the land with respect, your fellow hikers deserve your courtesy too. Keep an ear tuned to the trail behind you and allow faster hikers to pass ahead. On narrow trails give hikers coming uphill the right of way. When meeting horseback riders or pack animals, step off the trail on the uphill side and stand quietly till they pass. Take care to not dislodge rocks on scree slopes and headwalls, and yell out a warning to those below if a rock does break loose. Never throw rocks from atop cliffs or waterfalls.

Pitch your tent at least 100 metres from the trail, other campers, lakes, and streams. This avoids concentrating use and also helps to preserve a sense of solitude and privacy in the backcountry. Keep noise to a minimum in camp.

Leave the bear bells at home. At best they scare deer, elk, and other watchable wildlife and annoy other hikers. At worst they create a false sense of security, encouraging the wearers to blunder down trails heedless of wind direction, odors, berry crops, noises off trail, and bear signs—each a factor worth noting when hiking in bear country. See the section on safety for suggestions on avoiding bear confrontations.

Hiking with Children

While writing this book, we hiked many of the trails included here with our two sons, Evan, a two year old, and Ben, who was just six months old.

For young children a hike can present them with moments of discovery around every corner.

Evan ran circles around us on the shorter hikes, while Ben rode happily in a backpack designed for carrying young children. On longer hikes, Evan rested in his own backpack between his stints of walking down the trail.

Overnight trips in the backcountry are not recommended with infants and toddlers due to the difficulty of carrying the children and all of the necessary equipment.

The key to hiking with kids is the adults' attitude. Lower your expectations, forget about distant destinations, and choose trails with plenty of close-at-hand nature such as wildflowers, insects, birds, and small mammals. Toddlers love to test their balance on downed logs, toss sticks into small streams, chase butterflies and spiders, and poke their noses into bright flowers. Older children enjoy wading in streams and ponds, skipping stones, climbing trees, and scrambling on boulders. Avoid trails along cliffs and canyon rims or beside roiling rivers. Also limit your time on cold, windy ridges or in bug-infested bogs, where young children are likely to become uncomfortable and irritable more quickly.

Remember to pack the essentials for each child: food and water or juice, diapers for infants (and a plastic bag to carry soiled ones out), a sweater or jacket, rain gear, sun screen, and a hat for shade or warmth depending on the season. An extra shirt and pair of pants comes in handy in wet weather or when Junior misjudges the leap to the next stepping stone.

Older kids want to help plan the outing, so let them look at the map, read about the area, and ask questions if you talk with a park ranger or information staff. Bring along an instamatic camera, inexpensive binoculars, or a magnifying glass for the kids.

Most of the day hikes in this book are well-suited to children. For starters, try Johnston Canyon and Consolation Lakes in Banff National Park; Valley of the Five Lakes, the Mona Lake Loop, and the Whistlers in Jasper National Park; the short route into Crandell Lake, Lineham Creek, and the Lakeshore Trail in Waterton Lakes National Park; and any of the trails at Vermilion, Dinosaur, Cypress Hills, and Fish Creek provincial parks.

Backpack trips with older children can be great adventures even on easier trails. Consider the Egypt Lake region in Banff for avid hikers; the Saturday Night Lake loop in Jasper; the Spruce Coulee Trail in Cypress Hills; Crandell or Bertha lakes in Waterton; and Chester Lake in Peter Lougheed Provincial Park.

Safety

Bears and other critters

All wild animals are potentially dangerous, but chief among most hikers' worries are bears. Alberta is bear country; nearly every hike in this book crosses bear habitat. Black bears are fairly widespread and are the most frequently seen species of bear. Grizzly bears are found only in the western mountains and foothills, and in parts of the northern forest. Grizzlies generally keep to the alpine and subalpine zones through the summer, but frequent valley bottoms during spring and fall. All bears are opportunists and will revisit places that provided good food in the past. Ground squirrel colonies and berry patches are favourite dining areas. Grizzlies also like browsing through the dense vegetation usually found on avalanche paths.

When hiking in bear country, stay alert. Watch for tracks or droppings on the trail, dug out gopher holes, and ripped apart ant logs. Heed the wind. If you're walking into it a bear may not be able to smell or hear you coming.

Test the breeze with your own nose to detect carrion, a food cache, or possibly the pungent "wet dog" odor of a bear. Listen for noises off trail—the clatter of a large animal moving through brush, the mewing of a cub, or the warning cough of an annoyed adult. In dense brush or near rushing water, talk or sing loudly, whistle, or clap your hands repeatedly. Don't let small children stray far ahead or lag behind on the trail. And leave your dog at home. Dogs have been known to enrage bears only to come running back to their owners with the bear in hot pursuit.

Camping in bear country requires special precautions. Remember that you're protecting the safety of future campers as well as your own. Keep a clean camp. Cook and eat downwind from the sleeping area, at least 100 metres from the tents, and promptly clean up any mess or food scraps. Avoid smelly foods such as fresh meat and fish and drain cooking water well away from any likely tent sites. Hang your food in a sturdy bag or pack between two trees at least four metres from the ground and one metre from either tree. If possible, hang food 300 metres or more from camp. Put any clothes worn while cooking, all cookware, garbage, and even tubes of toothpaste in the bag. Deodorants, perfumes, and scented soaps are best left at home.

Pitch your tent near a tree if possible, and avoid sites altogether if they are near a noisy stream, an animal path, or any fresh bear sign. Keep a strong flashlight in the tent for any forays around camp in the dark. Never hike at night.

Following all of these safeguards should promise a good night's sleep and days of uneventful hiking. Most people never see a bear, let alone confront one, but you may one day encounter a bear. Remember that each bear is an individual, unpredictable, and potentially dangerous. At the time, it may also help to know that most bear sightings pass without incident.

When hiking in bear country, stay alert.

Detour around the bear if possible, or retreat to the trailhead. Always leave the bear an escape route and do not run or scream. Running may trigger an attack and a healthy adult bear can run faster than a horse—you cannot outrun a bear, even over short distances.

If the bear is close, stay calm and watch its behaviour. Bears are naturally curious and may not appear in a hurry to leave. A bear may stand on its hind legs to get a better look and to pick up your scent. Stand still and speak in a low, non-threatening voice. An aggressive bear may snap its jaws together, bark or cough, or lower its head with the ears laid back. When faced with an aggressive bear, try to retreat slowly and quietly.

If the bear becomes agitated, stand your ground. Bears sometimes bluff by charging, then stopping short or veering away. Most actual attacks occur when a bear is surprised, either a sow with cubs or a bear protecting its food. Such attacks can happen quite suddenly, with little warning.

There are three strategies for coping with a full-fledged attack, but none of them is guaranteed and no one can predict which one will work best with any given bear. Every bear encounter is unique and demands a quick and often irrevocable decision. Climb a tree if one is handy, remembering that black bears are fast climbers and may come up after you. Adult grizzlies usually will not climb, but can reach over four metres high. Drop your pack or a piece of clothing before climbing the tree to distract the bear. If the bear is already upon you, drop to the ground and play dead. Put your forehead to your knees and clasp your hands behind your neck. Leave your pack on and try to protect your face and abdomen, rolling with the blows while remaining curled in a ball. Finally, you can fight back, though this should be considered a last resort. Grizzlies are often enraged by a counterattack, while black bears might be intimidated. All bears are remarkably powerful and quick; an attack can easily overwhelm even the strongest person. Use any weapon or shield at hand and yell for help.

Finally, keep in mind that bears are animals, after all, not human-hunting monsters. Most of the time, they are preoccupied with finding food and conserving energy. Both of these aims are best served by avoiding people, which most bears do extremely well. Consider yourself lucky if you see a bear in the wild, and enjoy the experience at a safe, respectful distance.

Other animals may also pose a hazard to backcountry travellers. Cougar attacks are rare but have increased in recent years, most frequently targeting small children or pets. Even rarer are confrontations with rabid or injured coyotes, wolves, skunks, and squirrels. During the rut, bull moose and elk become especially cantankerous and aggressive. Bison may also charge if approached too closely, and the females of all ungulates will bite and kick to protect their young. Photographers sometimes underestimate the ferocity and speed of grazing animals; invest in a telephoto lens and give them all a wide berth.

Drinking water

The old days of cupping your hands in a mountain stream and drinking deep are gone. An intestinal parasite, *Giardia lamblia*, has been widely dispersed by its hosts (primarily beaver, canines, and humans) and now lives in many coldwater streams and lakes across North America. *Giardia*

Even the clear, cold waters of a lake may contain the parasite Giardia lamblia.

symptoms first appear after an incubation period of several days to three weeks. They include stomach cramps, prolific gas, and diarrhea. If left untreated, dehydration, fatigue, and weight loss result. In chronic cases, internal organs may be damaged.

To avoid the disease, all drinking water should be boiled for at least five minutes or filtered through an approved water purifier. Several of the better backpacking filters on the market have proven track records for straining out water-borne bacteria and other contaminants. Iodine and chlorine tablets do not work consistently and produce their own unpleasant side effects if used repeatedly.

No treatment system is failsafe, so if symptoms appear see a doctor immediately.

Lost. . . and found again

Most of the trails in this book are easy to follow, particularly after reading the descriptions and scanning the maps. Hikers with limited experience should try the shorter day hikes before venturing deeper into the backcountry. Register with the park staff or leave your itinerary with family or friends if you plan to camp in the backcountry or undertake any risks such as river fords, glacier travel, or rock climbing. To stay on track in unfamiliar territory, take a topographic map and compass and refer to them frequently, *before* becoming disoriented. When passing an unmarked trail junction or ill-defined stretch of trail, glance back the way you've travelled to see how it will look on the return trip. Watch for landmarks and pay attention to stream drainage patterns and the lay of ridgelines.

If you do get lost, stay calm and take your bearings. Is there a stream or landform to use as a handrail back the way you came? Can you see any familiar landmarks? If not, find a cozy spot nearby and make yourself comfortable to wait until help arrives (which will be quicker in coming if you filed an itinerary with someone). Many people have survived a night or two in the wild and walked out on their own with the rescue party. A few have been carried out—in poor condition or worse—after wandering aimlessly, risking exhaustion and injury.

Hypothermia

Alberta's weather can change suddenly, and temperatures can drop unexpectedly even on the hottest summer day. Be aware of the danger of hypothermia, especially in the mountains and far north. Exposure to wind, cold, and moisture quickly robs the unprotected hiker of vital body heat, resulting in numb, clumsy hands, slurred speech, a stumbling gait, and loss of judgment. Exhaustion follows as the body loses its ability to reheat itself through shivering or continued exercise. Without immediate treatment, hypothermia is a killer.

The best cure is prevention, so always pack a water resistant windshell or raincoat and an insulating layer. Wool, polypropylene, and some other synthetics retain more of their insulating value when wet than most fabrics. Also carry a snack—fruit, a sandwich, or a candy bar—even on the shortest day hike. On overnight trips, carry a rain proof shelter, a good sleeping bag, and rain gear to cover yourself from head to toe.

Before you hit the trail

Plan your trip. Write or call for further information and up-to-the-minute trail conditions. If you can, avoid holidays and other high-use periods. Plan for an optional hike if the first choice must be postponed.

Assess the abilities of your hiking companions. Choose hikes appropriate for the weakest member of your party and set a reasonable pace. Select destinations and daily distances suited to your fitness level. Know your own limits. Unless you are a highly experienced hiker, do not hike alone and don't stray from the trail.

Check the weather report before you go. Change your itinerary or pack clothes, food, and shelter accordingly.

Leave your dog at home or with friends. Dogs chase wildlife, are carriers of *Giardia*, and may incite a bear to attack if one is encountered.

When leaving your car at the trailhead, roll the windows completely shut, take all money and valuables with you, and don't stash the keys under the bumper or atop a tire. Double check that all doors are locked before you start up the trail. Trailhead crime is rare in Alberta, but cases do crop up, and nothing ruins a great hiking trip like a burglarized or missing car. Report any vandalism or theft immediately to the R.C.M.P. or park ranger, and also to your insurance agent.

Pack all necessary medications in a handy pocket. People allergic to insect stings should carry Ana-kits or other interventions prescribed by their doctor. Make sure all medications are up to date. Let other people in your party know of your condition and where the medicine is stored.

Brush up on map and compass skills, and take a first aid course with your hiking companions.

Put a fresh roll of film in your camera, check the batteries, and clean the lens. Pack a spare roll or two of film.

Finally, lace up your boots and fill that water bottle. You're ready to hike. Enjoy!

Wonder Pass. Randy Roch photo

THE HIKES

Banff National Park

In 1887, just fifteen years after Yellowstone became the world's first national park, Banff was designated as Canada's first national park. Today Banff is the premier tourist attraction in Canada, host to more than three million visitors each year. Many of these people venture onto Banff's 1,500 kilometres of trails, making the backcountry here busier than any other area in Alberta.

Trails range from short, easy interpretive walks to extended loops through rugged, remote wilderness. Many hikes lead to shimmering alpine lakes, windy passes, and glacier-clad peaks. Wildflowers are abundant here from June through August, and backcountry travellers may see a wide variety of wildlife, from moose, elk, and deer to coyotes, wolves, and bears.

Anyone planning to camp in the backcountry must first obtain a backcountry use permit from a visitor information centre in the park. Permits can be requested by mail from the Park Superintendent, Banff National Park, Box 900, Banff, Alberta, TOL OCO. Include the number of people in your party, your destination, the proposed route, and the dates you plan to be in the backcountry.

HIKE 1   *AYLMER PASS*

General description: A strenuous day hike or overnighter to a high alpine pass on the boundary of the Ghost River Wilderness.
General location: On the north shore of Lake Minnewanka northeast of the Banff townsite in Banff National Park.
Maps: 82 O/6.
Special attractions: Spectacular views of Lake Minnewanka, Mount Aylmer, and the Palliser and Fairholme mountain ranges; abundant wildlife.
For more information: Park Superintendent, Banff National Park, P.O. Box 900, Banff, Alberta, TOL OCO. Ph: (403) 762-3324.
Finding the trailhead: To find the trailhead, exit the Trans Canada Highway at the east interchange for the town of Banff and follow the Lake Minnewanka Road north for about six kilometres to the lake. Park in the lot above the entrance to the tour boat concession.

The hike: Although strong hikers can do Aylmer Pass and the return trip as a day hike, most would find it far more rewarding to establish a base camp for a night or two on the shore of Lake Minnewanka. Total distance from the trailhead to the pass is fourteen kilometres. Due to southern exposure and low elevation on much of the trail, this is an excellent early or late season hike.

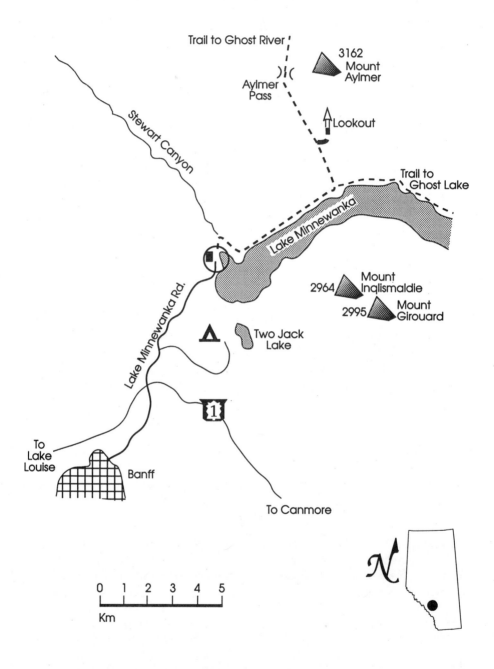

Walk around the concessioner's gate and down the paved limited-access road, past the boat concession and a picnic area. The trail begins at the end of the pavement, about one-half kilometre from the gate. The trail immediately doglegs into Stewart Canyon and crosses an impressive wooden truss bridge. A side trail cuts along the slope up the canyon, offering a chance for some exploratory wandering. The main trail switchbacks uphill through the trees before breaking into the open above the lake. The next six kilometres roll gently above the lake to the junction with the Aylmer Pass trail. A number of good tent sites can be found between this junction and the lake.

If you are setting up a base camp, consider spending the remainder of this first day hiking east along the lake, enjoying the gravel beaches and views across the lake to Mount Inglismaldie and Mount Girouard, both just under 3,000 metres.

Plan a full day to hike the remaining six kilometres to the pass. The trail gains nearly 700 metres in elevation over less than four kilomteres, and even in early June the sun can wither hikers on these south-facing slopes. Take plenty of drinking water.

Two kilometres into the climb a trail breaks right to the Aylmer fire lookout tower, about one and a half kilometres distant. The tower is no longer used, but offers fine views of the lake and surrounding mountains from an elevation of 2,040 metres. Also look for bighorn sheep on the open ridge around the tower.

The pass route continues to the left of the fire lookout junction, steadily climbing to treeline and the alpine zone. Sheep frequent the pass, and look for mountain goats on Mount Aylmer. The 3,162 metre summit of Mount Aylmer is a strenuous but uncomplicated scramble for those with a stout heart and sturdy shoes.

If you want to explore the Ghost River Wilderness beyond the pass, a detailed map and compass are handy. The trail is less defined as it drops into Spectral Creek Basin, but several routes follow the headwaters of the creek down to the Ghost River. The densely timbered basin is not heavily used by hikers and provides home range to grizzlies, black bear, elk, and wolverines. For more information about the Ghost River Wilderness Area, write to the Regional Director of Alberta Recreation and Parks, West Central Region, P.O. Box 920, Rimbey, Alberta, TOC 2JO.

HIKE 2   *TUNNEL MOUNTAIN*

General description: An easy walk from downtown Banff to the summit of Tunnel Mountain.

General location: Above downtown Banff in Banff National Park.

Maps: See the brochure "Banff and Vicinity Drives and Walks" available from the Park Information Centre at 224 Banff Avenue. Also: Banff 82 0/4.

Special attractions: Views of the entire townsite, Vermillion Lakes, Mount Rundle, and the Bow River Valley.

HIKE 2 *TUNNEL MOUNTAIN*

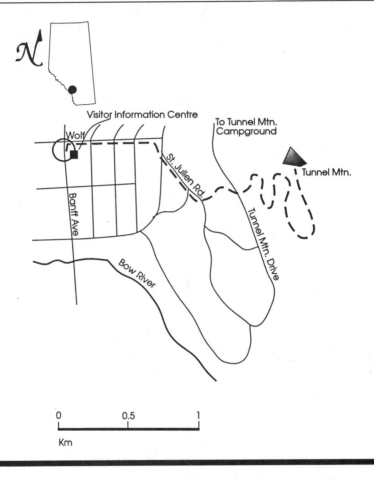

For more information: Park Superintendent, Banff National Park, P.O. Box 900, Banff, Alberta, T0L 0C0. Ph: (403) 762-3324.

Finding the trailhead: The entire hike, roundtrip, is five kilometres. From the Park Information Centre on Banff Avenue, follow Wolf Street east to St. Julien Road. Continue to the right up St. Julien for another 300 metres to the parking lot and trail sign on the uphill side of the road.

The hike: After a few hours of browsing in the museums and busy shops of downtown Banff, you can clear both mind and lungs on this easy stroll through the lodgepole pines and Douglas fir. The summit opens up 300 metres above town, with views of the surrounding valley and mountains. When hiking this popular, well-maintained trail, remember to make way for faster hikers and refrain from cutting the switchbacks.

The trail climbs to Tunnel Mountain Drive, crosses the road, and begins a series of looping switchbacks up the flank of Tunnel Mountain. Watch for deer along the trail, as well as Canada jays, dark-eyed juncoes, and nuthatches in the shade of the trees. Eventually the trail traverses the summit ridge heading north to a small knoll, once the site of a fire lookout tower. This point offers unobstructed views of the town and 2,949 metre Mount Rundle looming over the Bow River Valley.

HIKE 3   *EGYPT LAKE*

General description: An easy three- or four-day backpack to a lake-filled plateau set against the Continental Divide.
General location: Midway between Banff and Lake Louise on the western boundary of Banff National Park.
Maps: Banff National Park; Banff 82 O/4.
Special attractions: Extensive subalpine meadows, numerous lakes and peaks, fishing.
For more information: Park Superintendent, Banff National Park, P.O. Box 900, Banff, Alberta, TOL OCO. Ph: (403) 762-3324.
Finding the trailhead: From the Trans Canada Highway (1) west of Banff, turn west onto the Sunshine Ski Area access road and drive ten kilometres to the lower gondola station. Park in the large lot behind the station; the trail begins on a narrow gravel road cutting to the right up the slope behind the map kiosk.

The hike: Many hikers are first attracted to the Egypt Lake area by the mysterious names clustered in this corner of the park—Pharaoh Peaks, Mummy and Scarab lakes, the Whistling Valley, and Shadow Lake. Whistling Valley is named for the cries of the hoary marmots who live in the boulder fields there, but the story behind the Egyptian motif has been long lost. Nevertheless, this subalpine paradise is filled with wondrous features—shining lakes, snow-covered mountains, and luminous wildflowers—enough to warrant a week of exploring.

By driving to the Sunshine gondola station, the Healy Pass approach to Egypt Lake allows hikers to start nearly 300 metres higher in elevation than the Redearth Creek trailhead. This approach is also seven kilometres shorter than the route up Redearth and Pharaoh creeks.

From the end of the Sunshine access road, the trail follows an old gravel road for 800 metres before cutting to the right on a wide track into the trees above Healy Creek. After climbing through this dense, damp forest and crossing Healy Creek on a stout bridge, the trail levels off and narrows to a footpath that wanders through scrubby avalanche runouts and bands of fir and spruce.

About five kilometres in, the trail passes the ruins of an old cabin near the creek. Five hundred metres further the trail threads through the Healy Creek Campground, complete with picnic tables and a bear cable for hanging food. The Simpson Pass Trail joins the main track about 300 metres above the campground—turn right and begin the climb toward Healy Pass.

A second junction with the Simpson Pass loop appears just as the trail forges into open stands of alpine larch and meadows carpeted in wildflowers. Follow the main path to the right and up to a shallow stream crossing in the meadow below the Ramparts and the 2,904 metre Monarch to the south.

The rise over Healy Pass is straightforward and then the trail descends steadily for three kilometres to the multiple trail intersection at the meadow between the warden's cabin and the Egypt Lake Campground. The campground lies twelve kilometres from the trailhead at the Sunshine Gondola and includes a hiker's hut with a sixteen-person capacity. Hikers can reserve bunk space by registering at the visitor information centre in Banff. Its central location serves as an excellent base camp for day hiking into the Pharaoh and Whistling valleys or to Mummy and Scarab lakes. Plan to spend at least two nights at Egypt Lake.

Don't be surprised if the campground is busy with other backpackers; those wishing more privacy should consider the strenuous four kilometre climb to Talc Lake on the British Columbia side of Redearth Pass. The most popular options for leaving the basin include a traverse of the pass into spectacular Whistling Valley or descending the more mundane Pharaoh Creek drainage.

The trail through Whistling Valley takes off from the Egypt Lake junction, climbing a steep series of switchbacks up the south flank of Pharaoh Peaks to a meadow above Scarab Lake. Bear right at the juncture with the Scarab Lake side trail, continuing over the open pass and down a boulder strewn slope to the wetlands above Haiduk Lake. Views here are good down the length of the valley, with Haiduk Peak looming over the lake and ice-clad Mount Ball rising in the distance. The trail contours around the east shore of Haiduk Lake, then crosses to the west bank of the outlet stream before joining the Shadow Lake Trail nine kilometres from Egypt Lake. Most hikers pass the campsite at this junction and continue north five kilometres to Shadow Lake and the campground one kilometre below the lake. From here it is a thirteen-kilometre walk down Redearth Creek, ten kilometres of which are an old fire road, to the trailhead on the Trans Canada Highway. This loop, from the Sunshine gondola to the Redearth trailhead, totals forty kilometres.

The Pharaoh Creek trail offers a shorter exit from Egypt Lake, dropping through the larch and open meadows along the creek, with good views of the eastern flank of the Pharaoh Peaks. Four kilometres from the Egypt Lake warden's cabin, the trail passes Pharaoh Creek Campground and then crosses the stream and enters the forest for the remainder of the hike. The trail joins the Redearth Creek trail just below an outfitters cabin (unavailable for hikers), eleven kilometres from the trailhead. Turn right and follow the old fire road to the trailhead on the Trans Canada Highway. Using the Pharaoh Creek cutoff, the distance from the Sunshine gondola to the Redearth trailhead is thirty-two kilometres.

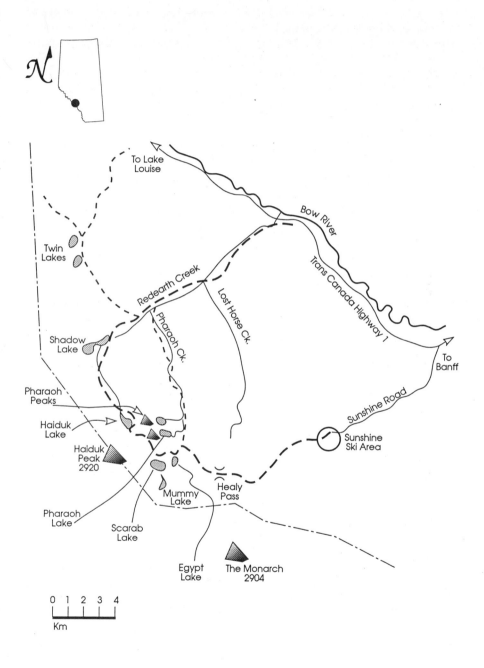

To Lake Louise

Bow River

Trans Canada Highway 1

Twin Lakes

Redearth Creek

Lost Horse Ck.

Pharaoh Ck.

Shadow Lake

To Banff

Pharaoh Peaks

Haiduk Lake

Sunshine Road

Sunshine Ski Area

Haiduk Peak 2920

Mummy Lake

Healy Pass

Pharaoh Lake

Scarab Lake

Egypt Lake

The Monarch 2904

0 1 2 3 4
Km

HIKE 4 *JOHNSTON CANYON*

General description: An easy day hike through a sinuous canyon to a set of colourful coldwater springs.

General location: South of Castle Junction on Highway 1-A in Banff National Park.

Maps: Banff National Park; Banff 82 O/4, Castle Mountain 82 O/5.

Special attractions: Deep, narrow canyon with numerous waterfalls; an ingeniously engineered trail projecting from the side of the canyon wall; colourful coldwater springs.

For more information: Park Superintendent, Banff National Park, P.O. Box 900, Banff, Alberta, TOL OCO. Ph: (403) 762-3324.

Finding the trailhead: From Banff, drive west on the Trans Canada Highway, turning north onto the Bow Valley Parkway, Highway 1-A. Drive about twenty kilometres north to the Johnston Canyon Campground. The parking lot is 300 metres further north on 1-A, on the east side of the road. Hikers staying at Johnston Canyon Campground can reach the trailhead by following the gravel trail on the north end of the campground, under the road culvert along Johnston Creek, to a large wooden bridge that crosses to the north bank below Johnston Creek Lodge.

The hike: Johnston Canyon is one of the busiest trails in Banff National Park, attracting throngs of sightseers who may not brave another trail in the park. To accommodate this heavy visitation, the trail is paved over its lower section, and railings run the length of the sections that cantilever out from the gorge's sheer walls. But the canyon's many waterfalls and water-carved chutes are well worth the jostling and traffic jams of the lower trail, and the upper reaches revert to the more customary dirt footpath before reaching Johnston Meadow and the Ink Pot Springs.

The lower trail stays close to Johnston Creek, at times suspended directly over the stream, with frequent interpretive displays and vantage points. Two kilometres from the trailhead a spur trail leads down to the lower falls. Be sure to cross the bridge and scurry through the short tunnel to the mist-filled grotto at the base of the falls.

The trail climbs more seriously toward the thirty-metre upper falls, passing numerous smaller falls along the way and occasionally winding into the woods at the canyon's rim. The upper falls are reached at the three kilometre mark, and just beyond the trail joins the dirt road from Moose Meadows. Bear right along the road as it climbs above the upper canyon until it narrows to a single track again and descends to Johnston Meadow and the Ink Pots. These coldwater springs run year-round at four degrees Celsius and feed into Johnston Creek. Most day hikers stop here for lunch, then retrace their steps back to the trailhead.

To avoid the return trip down Johnston Canyon, hikers can proceed 200 metres past the Ink Pots, across the bridge over Johnston Creek to the junction with the trail down to Hillsdale Meadow. It is eight kilometres to the Bow Valley Parkway along this forested trail, arriving at the trailhead

HIKE 4 *JOHNSTON CANYON*

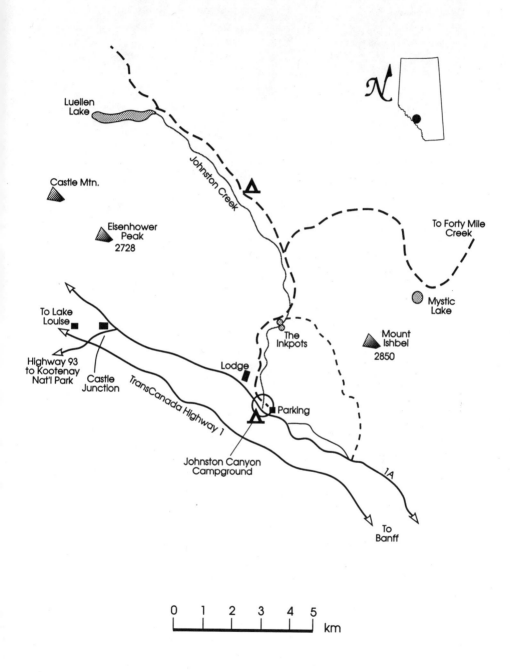

The lower falls on Johnston Creek

some four kilometres south of Johnston Creek Lodge. For those wishing to stay overnight, a backcountry campsite lies in the trees just beyond the Ink Pots. A less populated campsite at Luellen Lake—twelve kilometres further up Johnston Creek toward Pulsatilla Pass—is available for hikers seeking solitude and good fishing.

HIKE 5 *ROCKBOUND LAKE*

General description: A moderately strenuous day hike or overnight to a pair of high lakes nestled at the foot of sheer rock walls and talus piles.
General location: Behind Castle Mountain, just east of Castle Junction on the Trans Canada Highway in Banff National Park.
Maps: Banff National Park; Castle Mountain 82 O/5.
Special attractions: Two magnificent alpine lakes; ancient limestone faces of the Eisenhower Tower and Castle Mountain; views down the Bow Valley.

HIKE 5 *ROCKBOUND LAKE*

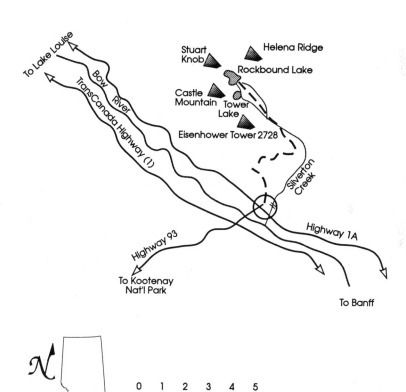

For more information: Park Superintendent, Banff National Park, P.O. Box 900, Banff, Alberta, TOL OCO. Ph: (403) 762-3324.

Finding the trailhead: From Banff, follow either the Trans Canada Highway or Bow Valley Parkway approximatley thirty kilometres west (north) to Castle Junction. If travelling on the Trans Canada Highway, turn east on the one-kilometre road that links the two highways. There is a paved parking lot at the trailhead next to the warden's home on the Bow Valley Parkway, 200 metres east of the shop and inn at Castle Junction.

The hike: Massive and multi-tiered, Castle Mountain attracts many admiring glances from drivers along this stretch of the Trans Canada Highway. Knowing that two lakes are hidden beyond its ramparts makes the mountain even more attractive for those eager to leave the pavement and traffic behind.

At first, the trail follows an old road up the southern slope of Castle Mountain. But the trail narrows to a single track after about five kilometres, and the 2,752 metre Eisenhower Tower comes into view. The Tower is an outcrop of the ancient limestone that formed these mountains. From here the trail parallels Silverthorn Creek, heading northwest into a small valley beneath the ramparts of Castle Mountain. This leg of the trail is boggy from snowmelt well into mid-summer. Look for glacier lilies and bog gentians here in the meadows before the lakes.

Eight kilometres into the hike, the trail arrives at Tower Lake, a small tarn with trees and meadow on one side and sheer limestone cliffs rising above the other. The trail skirts the lake to the right and climbs the rocky ridge. On top, Rockbound Lake comes into view—a fair-sized saucer of water completely surrounded by rock. The two lakes are slightly less than one kilometre apart.

There are good tent sites in the scattered subalpine forest between the two lakes, and the open country around Rockbound Lake offers ample room for exploring. A scramble partway up the northern flanks of Castle Mountain or an easy walk up the slopes of Helena Ridge to the northeast gives a better view of the basin, and the numerous boulders and small ledges ringing the upper lake offer opportunities to practice climbing skills for those with the proper equipment.

HIKE 6   *TWIN LAKES*

General description: A moderate one- or two-night backpack to a pair of high lakes nestled in nearly identical settings against the eastern face of Storm Mountain.

General location: Southwest of Castle Junction on the western border of Banff National Park.

Maps: Banff National Park; Banff 82 O/4; Mount Goodsir 82 N/1.

Special attractions: Vista, Arnica, and Twin lakes; splendid views of Storm Mountain and the divide range.

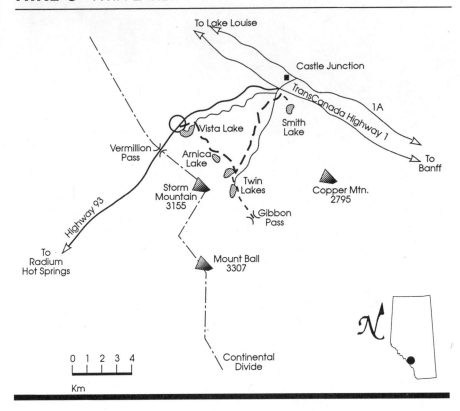

For more information: Park Superintendent, Banff National Park, P.O. Box 900, Banff, Alberta, TOL OCO. Ph: (403) 762-3324.

Finding the trailhead: From Castle Junction, drive west on Highway 93 for eight kilometres to the Vista Lake viewpoint. The viewpoint is a large parking area on the south side of the road overlooking the 1968 Vermillion Pass burn. The trail is marked with a sign and drops quickly from the southeast corner of the parking lot.

The hike: Most veteran backpackers own stout hearts and sore knees, giving credence to the old rule that you go uphill with your heart and come down with your knees. With this in mind, you will find the ascent to Twin Lakes a genuine workout, while the retreat back down to civilisation is more gradual and forgiving. And the destination—Twin Lakes—more than rewarding for your efforts.

From the Vista Lake viewpoint, look south over the lake and the low ridge beyond to scan the first several kilometres of the route. The trail descends quickly over the first 1.5 kilometres to the shore of Vista Lake, crosses a bridge over the outlet stream on the lake's eastern end, and then begins climbing at a moderate pitch. One kilometre further a side trail from the Storm Mountain Lodge joins the main track. Bear right and continue the

Vista Lake with the route to Twin Lakes in the background.

uphill grunt as it steepens. This is the hottest, most tedious part of the climb, open to the sun until the trail leaves the burn and enters the shady forest.

The trail soon levels off before dipping slightly to Arnica Lake, five kilometres from the trailhead. The talus slopes and cliffs of Storm Mountain provide a dramatic backdrop to Arnica Lake, which is also a popular day hike destination for anglers hoping to land one of the lake's cutthroat trout.

Leaving Arnica, the trail scales an outlying ridge from Storm Mountain, reaching 2,285-metre Arnica Summit in a strenuous 800 metre push. From here, it is little over a kilometre down to Upper Twin Lake and the designated campsites. Both of the Twin Lakes are set against the cliffs and snowfields of the Continental Divide, ringed by subalpine forest laced with alpine larch. Total distance from Vista Lake viewpoint is eight kilometres.

If you have arranged a shuttle or are willing to hitch hike back to your car, leave the Twin Lakes basin by dropping to the trail junction below the lower lake and turn left. Follow this gradually descending trail through meadows and larch parklands, over a marshy section plagued with roots and rocks, down to the Altrude Creek picnic area, a distance of eight kilometres. Near the trailhead, the trail crosses Altrude Creek and joins an old quarry road for the final 500 metres.

HIKE 7   *PLAIN-OF-SIX-GLACIERS*

General description: An easy day hike with a moderate climb just before the turnaround point.
General location: From the Chateau at Lake Louise in Banff National Park.
Maps: Banff National Park; Lake Louise 82 N/8.
Special attractions: Six active glaciers, frequent avalanches observable from a safe distance, a backcountry teahouse, and mountain goats.
For more information: Park Superintendent, Banff National Park, P.O. Box 900, Banff, Alberta, TOL OCO. Ph: (403) 762-3324.
Finding the trailhead: To get to the trailhead, take the Lake Louise exit on the Trans Canada Highway and follow the signs on the spur road for Lake Louise. Park in the visitor lot for the chateau and follow the asphalt path to the lake's eastern shore.

The hike: The trail to the Plain-of-six-glaciers is one of the more heavily used routes within Banff National Park. But trails become popular with good reason, and this particular hike offers several rewards.

The trail wraps around the northern shore of Lake Louise and is paved until it leaves the water's edge for the gradual ascent toward the Plain-of-six-glaciers.

Within two kilometres from the chateau the trail begins to climb, but the grade steepens notably only after the junction with the Mirror Lake highline trail roughly three kilometres into the hike. Over the next 2.5 kilometres the trail twists up the side of this glacier-scoured valley in a series of switchbacks, rewarding the hiker with views of Mount Victoria and Mount Lefroy with each turn in the trail.

At 5.5 kilometres the trail levels off just below a two-story teahouse where fresh squeezed lemonade and home baked muffins tempt hikers to while away the afternoon. But the trail continues, skittering along the crest of a lateral moraine for another kilometre to a precarious rockpile below Abbot's Pass. Mountain goats sometimes lounge on the grassy ledges above the trail. This is also a good vantage point for scanning the surrounding glaciers for avalanches or for watching the progress of climbing parties approaching the stone hut atop the pass.

The return trip to Chateau Lake Louise takes about two hours unless you opt to follow the Mirror Lake highline trail. The highline trail is often less crowded, but requires additional climbing before dropping back down toward Lake Louise. This route also adds about four kilometres to the roundtrip distance.

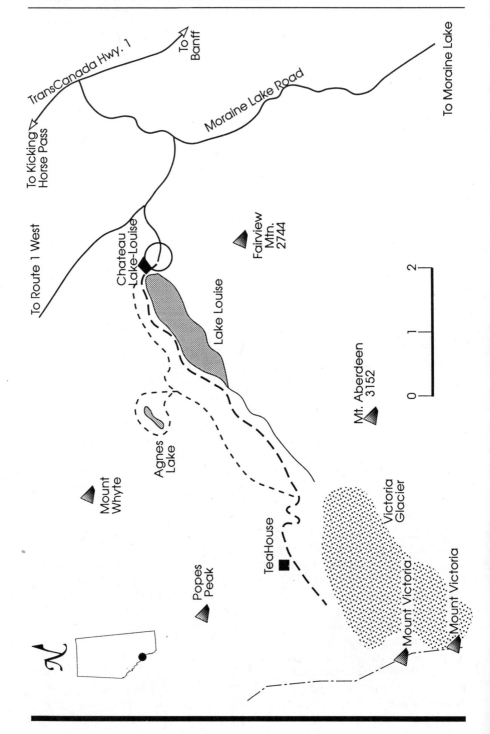

HIKE 8 *CONSOLATION LAKES*

General description: An easy half-day stroll through a subalpine forest to a pair of sparkling lakes below the walls of Bident Mountain.
General location: South of Lake Louise in Banff National Park.
Maps: Banff National Park; Lake Louise 82 N/8.
Special attractions: Views of Bident Mountain, Mount Quadra, and Mount Temple; Babel Creek, Lower and Upper Consolation Lakes.
For more information: Park Superintendent, Banff National Park, P.O. Box 900, Banff, Alberta, TOL OCO. Ph: (403) 762-3324.
Finding the Trailhead: From the Lake Louise access road, follow the Moraine Lake Road eleven kilometres to the parking lot at the end of the road. The trail begins on the boardwalk next to the picnic area below Moraine Lake. Look for the sign mentioning the Moraine Lake overlook and Consolation Lakes.

The hike: The Consolation Valley was named in counterpoint to Desolation Valley, the original label pinned to the raw, boulder strewn canyon above Moraine Lake now known as Wenkchemna Valley. And the short, shady,

HIKE 8 *CONSOLATION LAKES*

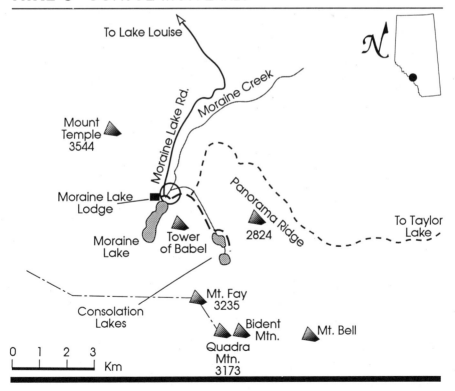

Bident Mountain towers above Lower Consolation Lake.

gently graded trail into Consolation Lakes should well console weary hikers. No other trail in the park requires as little effort to reach such a gem of an alpine lake basin.

The trail begins as boardwalk leaving the Moraine Lake picnic area. Bear left through the boulder field below Moraine Lake—a short side trail to the right climbs the rock pile for a view of the lake. After winding through the boulders, the main trail settles into a steady but easy ascent along Babel Creek through a spruce and fir forest.

As the trail rounds the foot of the Tower of Babel (a ridge running north from 3,101 metre Mount Babel), the grade eases and the noise of Babel Creek draws nearer. One kilometre from the trailhead, the trail to Taylor Lake forks off to the left, immediately crossing Babel Creek. Continue straight on the main trail for another kilometre to a small meadow along Babel Creek. Watch for moose and elk here, especially in the early morning. Just 500 metres more brings you to the mouth of a large ampitheatre with Lower Consolation Lake shimmering at the head of Babel Creek.

Pick your way across the boulder field on the west bank of the creek to reach the lower lake. To continue on to the upper lake, cross the stream by hopping boulders (in higher water a retreat downstream to a narrower section may be necessary) and follow the grassy path around the east shore of the lower lake. Cross the scree slope and climb the mounds of glacial debris separating the two lakes. The second lake affords a better vantage of Consolation Pass and Mount Bell to the south.

Although this trail attracts a good number of visitors, hikers seeking a sense of remoteness and solitude can still enjoy this trail at sunrise or sunset, particularly later in the season when the crowds have thinned.

HIKE 9 *WENKCHEMNA PASS*

General description: A moderate day hike into a remote glacial valley.
General location: Southwest of Lake Louise in Banff National Park.
Maps: Banff National Park; 82 N/8.
Special attractions: Moraine and Eiffel lakes and Valley of the Ten Peaks; an array of impressive, glacier-clad mountains.
For more information: Park Superintendent, Banff National Park, Box 900, Banff, Alberta TOL OCO. Ph: (403) 762-3324.
Finding the trailhead: To reach Moraine Lake and the trailhead, take the Lake Louise access road from the Trans Canada Highway. Within 3.5 kilometres, the road to Moraine Lake forks off to the left. This road ends in eleven kilometres at a large parking lot at the foot of the lake. Walk down to the lakeshore and past the lodge to the trailhead.

The hike: Wenkchemna Pass rises to just over 2,600 metres at the head of the Valley of Ten Peaks, so named because of the row of sawtoothed mountains forming the valley's southern wall. At the mouth of this valley, the peaks are mirrored in the turquoise waters of Moraine Lake, a popular tourist destination.

The trail to Wenkchemna Pass leaves the lakeshore path and steadily switchbacks for 2.5 kilometres to the junction with the Larch Valley Trail. Take it slow on the initial climb and don't shortcut the switchbacks—this is the steepest section of the trail and there's no point burning the thighs at the outset. The dense spruce and fir forest here shades the trail, easing the work

Moraine Lake from the trail to Wenkchemna Pass.

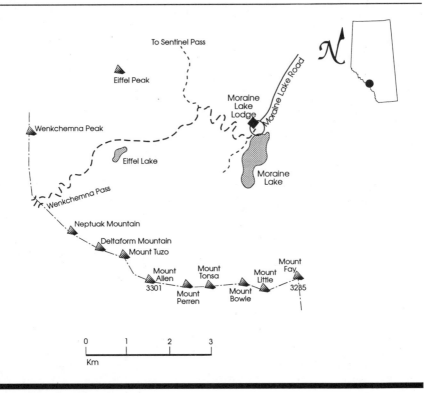

of gaining elevation.

At the Larch Valley junction, stay to the left on the level grade heading west. From here, the trail wends gradually out of the trees and across open slopes, always facing the jagged peaks across the valley. The rock-strewn Wenkchemna Glacier fills the valley floor, with Moraine Lake shining at the mouth. Listen for rockfalls and avalanches across the valley. Also keep an eye out for deer and bighorn sheep, and for bears browsing on the slopes along the trail.

Roughly six kilometres into the hike, the trail crosses a scree slope above Eiffel Lake and then traverses an old rockslide and fields of glacial cobble, at one point following the crest of an esker or small ridge of debris in the middle of the glacier's footprint. From here, several routes to the pass are possible, some marked by cairns of piled stones. Snow may linger on this final slope into July, longer in the gullies and on sections of the proper trail. The snow may offer good footing early in the day, providing a more direct approach to the pass.

Western winds often snarl over the saddle that marks the pass, but a scattering of boulders at the base of Wenkchemna Peak to the north offers a choice of sheltered lunch spots with views into remote regions of Yoho and Kootenay national parks. Mountains goats are common here—hikers may smell their musky scent before actually sighting one.

HIKE 10 *HECTOR LAKE*

General description: A short day hike—with a major river ford—to the shores of a large, glacier-fed lake in the Bow Valley.

General location: Just west of the Icefields Parkway, about eighteen kilometres north of the junction with the Trans Canada Highway in Banff National Park.

Maps: Banff National Park; Hector Lake 82 N/9.

Special attractions: Fishing, fording the Bow River, views of the Waputik Range and Balfour Pass.

For more information: Park Superintendent, Banff National Park, P.O. Box 900, Banff, Alberta, TOL OCO. Ph: (403) 762-3324.

Finding the trailhead: The trailhead is marked with a sign on the west side of the Icefields Parkway about one kilometre north of the Hector Lake

HIKE 10 *HECTOR LAKE*

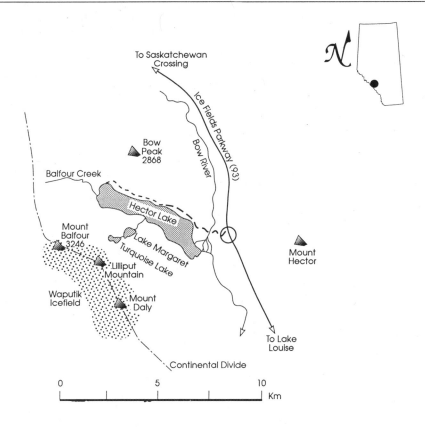

viewpoint. Park on the west side of the road along the widened shoulder. The trail begins at the north end of the pull out.

The hike: Although Hector Lake lies within two kilometres of the Icefields Parkway, few hikers visit its shores. The Bow River threads between the road and lake, presenting a dangerous ford when the water is high. **Fording the Bow should be attempted only by strong hikers with previous experience in crossing swift rivers, and then only during low water.** It is best to try this hike in late August, September, or October, but beware daily fluctuations in the river's flow. Glacier-fed rivers are usually at their lowest in the morning and tend to increase through the day as warmer temperatures add meltwater to the current. To the hiker, this means that a knee-deep stream may become a waist-high torrent by mid-afternoon. Exercise caution.

For the first kilometre, the trail drops down onto the densely timbered Bow River floodplain. The route is muddy and potholed much of the distance to the river, partly a symptom of the heavy use from people going to fish the Bow River. Don't stray off the trail just to keep your boots dry— such detours only lead to more widespread damage.

At low water, the river can be forded where the trail leads to the water's edge. If this looks risky, another ford can be found about fifty metres downstream where the channel splits around a small island. The current can be strong at either ford—if the water reaches your waist, turn back and be content to stroll the banks of the Bow.

If you manage to cross the river, proceed upstream along the bank to pick up the trail. From here, the trail enters the forest again for an easy one-kilometre walk to the cabins of an old outfitting camp on the eastern shore of Hector Lake. Pulpit Peak, Lilliput Mountain, and other peaks of the Waputik Range rise beyond the lake. Look for osprey and eagles in the crowns of trees ringing the shore. Also keep an eye—and ear—out for bear and moose, particularly in the brushy thickets along the Bow River.

HIKE 11 *PEYTO GLACIER*

General description: A strenuous day hike to the toe of a glacier spilling from the Waputik Icefield.
General location: Atop Bow Pass, forty-five kilometres north of Lake Louise on the Icefields Parkway in Banff National Park.
Maps: Banff National Park; Hector Lake 82 N/9.
Special attractions: Peyto Lake and Glacier.
For more information: Park Superintendent, Banff National Park, P.O. Box 900, Banff, Alberta, TOL OCO. Ph: (403) 762-3324.
Finding the trailhead: Turn west on the access road at the summit of Bow Pass and turn right into the large parking lot. An asphalt path leads 400 metres to the wooden deck of the viewpoint. Continue uphill about ten metres past the deck; the trail drops from here through a thick forest in a frenzy of switchbacks.

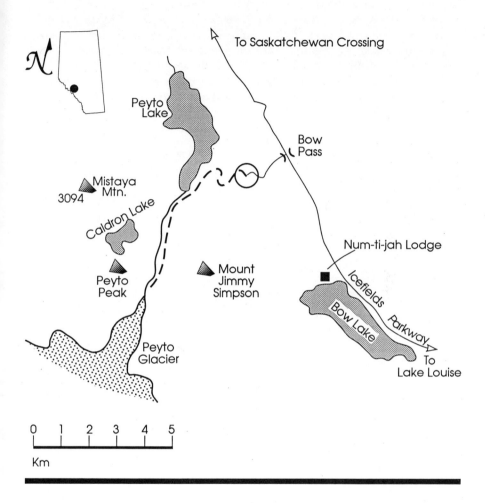

The hike: Each year, thousands of tourists stop at the viewpoint overlooking the turquoise waters of Peyto Lake. But few people venture beyond the 400-metre interpretive trail for a close-up look at the lake and the glacier that gives Peyto Lake its astonishing colour.

A set of switchbacks rapidly drops the trail from the viewpoint to the head of Peyto Lake in 2.5 kilometres of hiking.

At the bottom, a gravelly glacial plain flanks the inlet stream. Walk south across these flats, following the stream to where it cuts through a ridge of trees, actually an old moraine. About 100 metres to the left of the stream, the trail enters the trees and climbs the ridge, then continues south over the cobbles and glacial debris for another four kilometres to the toe of the glacier. Stone cairns mark most of this route as it follows the headwaters of the

Mistaya River to their source between Peyto Peak and Mount Jimmy Simpson.

The names of this region are a mixture of Indian and pioneer history. Mistaya is the Stoney Indian name for the "great" or grizzly bear. Peyto Lake was named after Bill Peyto, an early explorer of the area, and later the first superintendent of Banff National Park.

The final approach to the glacier is steep, with unstable footing. Don't attempt to climb on the glacier without proper equipment and know-how. And remember to save some time and energy for the demanding 2.5 kilometre climb from Peyto Lake back to the viewpoint at the end of the day. Also, carry plenty of drinking water for this trip. The stream and Peyto Lake are thick with sediment—the same "glacial flour" that colours the lake—and are not palatable without filtering or a lengthy settling.

Peyto Lake and the Mistaya River Valley.

HIKE 12 *SASKATCHEWAN GLACIER*

General description: A moderate day hike to the toe of the largest valley glacier of the Columbia Icefield.

General location: At the southern foot of Sunwapta Pass on the Icefields Parkway in Banff National Park.

Maps: Banff National Park; Columbia Icefield 83 C/3.

Special attractions: Headwaters of the North Saskatchewan River, and easy access to the rock and ice world of a massive glacier.

For more information: Park Superintendent, Jasper National Park, P.O. Box 10, Jasper, Alberta, TOE 1EO. Ph: (403) 852-6161.

Finding the trailhead: By road, the trailhead is roughly thirty-five kilometres north of the gas station at Saskatchewan Crossing or eleven kilometres south of the summit of Sunwapta Pass. An abandoned concrete bridge crosses the river just upstream of the new highway bridge; park along the shoulder of the abandoned access road above the old bridge.

The hike: Hiking the seven kilometres to the toe of the Saskatchewan Glacier is a small price to pay for an afternoon of exploring the raw edge of the ice and surrounding terrain. And unlike the Athabasca Glacier just over the Sunwapta Divide, crowds are uncommon at the headwaters of the North Saskatchewan River.

The trail begins on the Icefields Parkway about 500 metres below the big switchback at the southern foot of Sunwapta Pass. Walk across the old bridge and turn right, following the abandoned road and then the rough trail into the forest. Within 500 metres the trail joins an old access road that climbs

HIKE 12 *SASKATCHEWAN GLACIER*

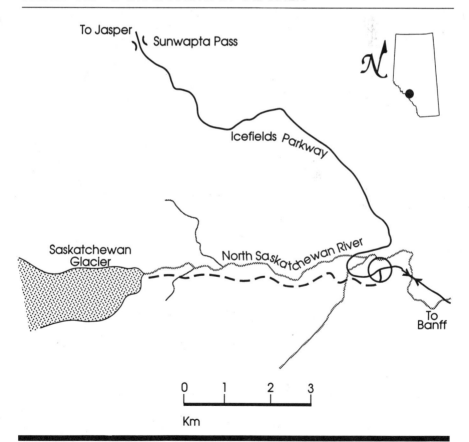

a low, wooded ridge and continues for another 2.5 kilometres along the glacier's outwash flats. In places the roadway has been washed out by the meandering river. A rocky track leads upstream along the southern bank, growing less defined as you near the glacier.

The final three kilometres cover rugged, untracked terrain, including several low moraines deposited as the glacier retreated up the valley. At the very toe of the glacier, meltwater sometimes turns the fine gravels and sand into a muck that is best avoided.

To scramble onto the glacier itself, look for an approach route on exposed bedrock. If you travel on the ice, take along ropes and ice axes, and be aware of crevasses and weak snow bridges.

HIKE 13   NIGEL PASS

General description: A moderately strenuous day hike to a timberline pass overlooking the wilderness of Jasper National Park's southern end.
General location: Near the border between Banff and Jasper national parks.
Maps: Banff National Park; Columbia Icefield 83 C/3.
Special attractions: Rolling alpine meadows, spectacular views of surrounding mountains.
For more information: Park Superintendent, Banff National Park, P.O. Box 900, Banff, Alberta, TOL OCO. Ph: (403) 762-3324.
Finding the trailhead: The trail begins just off the Icefields Parkway, about eight kilometres south of Sunwapta Pass or three kilometres north of the highway bridge over the North Saskatchewan River. Turn east on the short access road and park just above the locked gate.

The hike: Nigel Pass is a popular jumping off point for a number of extended backpack trips in the remote valleys of southern Jasper National Park (see the hike description for Brazeau Lake), but the climb to the pass can also serve as a rewarding day hike. The trail gains less than 400 metres of elevation in over seven kilometres, making the ascent to timberline less grueling than some other passes in the park.

From the gate, the trail drops down to Nigel Creek, crossed by a footbridge, and then contours to the northwest across a series of avalanche paths. Two kilometres into the hike, at an old indian hunting camp known as Camp Parker, the trail turns north toward the summit of Nigel Pass. The terrain becomes more open, offering views of Parker's Ridge and the peaks of the Columbia Icefield to the east. Nigel Pass, with a cairn marking the border between Banff and Jasper national parks, is reached after seven kilometres of steady climbing. Nigel Peak rises to 3,211 metres just west of the pass, and the chasm of the upper Brazeau Valley drops away to the north.

From the pass, more adventurous hikers can continue cross-country toward Cataract Pass to the southeast or by trail down the north side of Nigel Pass along one of the forks of the Brazeau River. Reserve plenty of daylight hours for the hike back, and take a raincoat or windbreaker and extra sweater as a precaution. The evening chill comes early to this high country, in part because of its proximity to the Columbia Icefield.

HIKE 13 *NIGEL PASS*

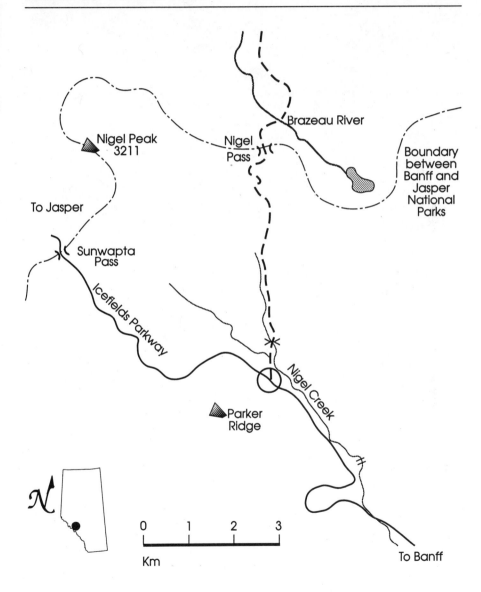

Looking southeast toward Cataract Pass from Nigel Pass.

Jasper National Park

The largest park in the Canadian Rockies is Jasper National Park, Banff's neighbor to the north. Jasper's 1,000 kilometres of trails offer a good variety of day hikes and backpack trips, with the balance in favour of extended treks through remote wilderness. Trails are less heavily used here than in Banff, although a few popular routes can be crowded during the height of the hiking season.

Jasper is famous for its wildlife: huge herds of elk, flocks of bighorn sheep, woodland caribou, moose, wolves, black and grizzly bears. Fall is the best time of year for observing these animals, when ungulates begin the rut and predators roam more boldly, preparing for winter.

Jasper operates a quota system on its backcountry trails in an effort to preserve the quality of the wilderness experience for visitors. If you plan to spend a night or more in the backcountry, you must first obtain a use permit. Quotas for busier trails can fill rapidly, particularly in July and August. Plan ahead and select several backup hikes. The park staff will also take reservations to fill up to thirty percent of each trail's quota. You may book a slot on a specific trail up to three weeks before your actual trip date by writing to the Park Superintendent, Jasper National Park, Box 10, Jasper, Alberta, TOE 1EO. In your request, include the number of people in your party, your destination, the proposed route, and the dates you plan to be in the backcountry.

HIKE 14   *BRAZEAU LAKE LOOP*

General description: A weeklong expedition into the remote wilds of the Rockies in Jasper National Park.
General location: East of the Columbia Icefield in southern Jasper National Park.
Maps: Jasper National Park, Columbia Icefield 83 C/3, Sunwapta Peak 83 C/6, Job Creek 83 C/7.
Special attractions: Solitude, abundant wildlife, several alpine passes, and Brazeau Lake, one of the largest backcountry lakes in the park.
For more information: Park Superintendent, Jasper National Park, P.O. Box 10, Jasper, Alberta, TOE 1EO. Ph: (403) 852-6161.
Finding the trailhead: Nigel Pass offers the best access to the Brazeau Lake region, providing a highly scenic beginning and end to the loop. The trailhead is found just off the Icefields Parkway, about eight kilometres south of Sunwapta Pass or three kilometres north of the highway bridge over the North Saskatchewan River. Turn east on the short access road and park just above the locked gate.

The hike: This eighty-kilometre loop is one of the premier backpack trips in the Canadian Rockies. The mountain scenery is spectacular, the trails are rugged but well marked, wildlife is abundant, and few people venture into this corner of the park. Strong hikers can do this loop in four days, but the scenery and four high passes entice many hikers to pace themselves over five to seven days.

After crossing Nigel Creek on a footbridge, the trail climbs steadily for seven kilometres to the 2,195 metre summit of Nigel Pass. Then the trail drops along the headwaters of the south fork of the Brazeau River, crossing the stream once and then descending steeply through old rockslides and open meadows. The first designated campsite, Boulder Creek Campground, occurs at about eleven kilometres, just after a bridge over the river. The Four Point Campground is another three kilometres down the trail, near the junction with the Jonas Pass trail.

Bear right at the Jonas Pass junction, following the Brazeau River downstream, again crossing the river on a bridge at the eighteen-kilometre mark. Roughly two kilometres beyond this bridge is the Wolverine South Campground, one of the more pleasant campsites along the route.

The trail continues to descend the forested valley, finally reaching the outlet of Brazeau Lake, the north fork of the Brazeau River, at twenty-nine kilometres. Turn left after crossing the bridge and follow the valley two

Jonas Pass area of the Brazeau Lake Loop

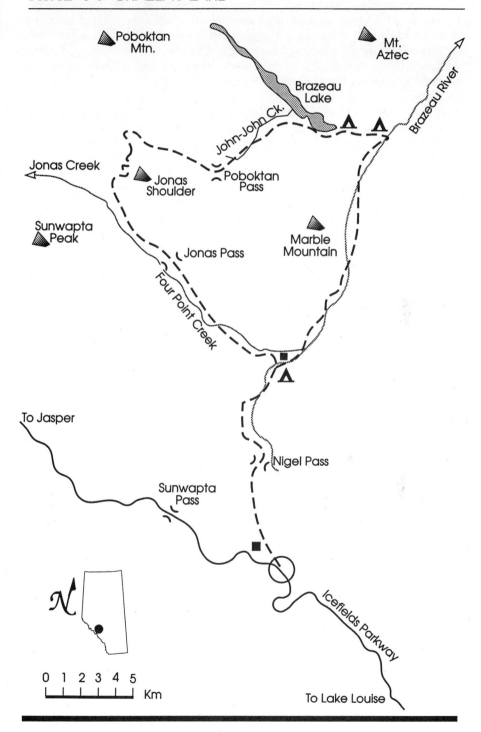

Poboktan
Mtn.

Brazeau
Lake

Mt.
Aztec

Brazeau River

John-John Ck.

Jonas Creek

Jonas
Shoulder

Poboktan
Pass

Sunwapta
Peak

Jonas Pass

Marble
Mountain

Four Point Creek

To Jasper

Nigel Pass

Sunwapta
Pass

Icefields Parkway

To Lake Louise

0 1 2 3 4 5
Km

kilometres, past the Poboktan Pass trail junction to the end of Brazeau Lake. There is a designated campsite 500 metres below the lake.

To complete the loop back to Nigel Pass, backtrack 500 metres to the Poboktan Pass junction, and head northwest. Within three kilometres the trail opens onto a large slide overlooking Brazeau Lake. Five kilometres further, after climbing through the narrow John-John Creek valley, the trail passes John-John Creek Campground. Poboktan Pass (2,300 metres) is reached in another four kilometres of steep climbing.

From the pass, the trail drops 200 metres in three kilometres to the Jonas Cutoff Campground at the intersection with the trail to Jonas Pass. Turn left—south—and follow this trail as it quickly regains timberline on the Jonas Shoulder, a 2,470-metre high ridge guarding the Jonas Creek drainage. This section of trail is one of the highest in the park and snowbanks may linger into August, sometimes obscuring the trail. On top, watch for marmots, mountain goats, grizzly bears, and caribou, all summer residents of this alpine paradise.

The trail drops sharply toward Jonas Creek, then turns southeast and gradually ascends 2,320 metre Jonas Pass, a long, wide summit surrounded by jagged peaks and massive snowfields. Dropping sharply once again, the trail follows Four Point Creek the remaining ten kilometres to the junction with the Brazeau River trail at Four Point Campground.

Turn right on the Brazeau River trail and retrace your steps from days ago, climbing Nigel Pass for a last glimpse of the Brazeau region before returning to the trailhead along the Icefields Parkway.

HIKE 15 *WILCOX PASS*

General description: An easy day hike to a broad alpine pass with stunning views of the Columbia Icefield.

General location: Above the Columbia Icefield Visitor Centre near the border between Banff and Jasper national parks.

Maps: 83 C/3 and 83 C/6.

Special attractions: High alpine terrain with spectacular views of the mountains, snowfields, and glaciers of the Columbia Icefield.

For more information: Park Superintendent, Jasper National Park, Box 10, Jasper, Alberta T0E 1E0. Ph: (403) 852-6161.

Finding the trailhead: The trailhead is easy to find, just off the Icefields Parkway on the access road to the Wilcox Creek Campground, one kilometre north of Sunwapta Pass or two kilometres south of the Columbia Icefield Visitor Centre.

The hike: This eleven-kilometre day hike offers more than its share of alpine scenery, yet the hike itself is not too demanding, particularly if you stop for lunch on top. Take along a warm hat and jacket—even in mid-summer days can be cool and wind or rain raises the risk of hypothermia.

Until the turn of the century, glaciers filled the valley where the Icefields

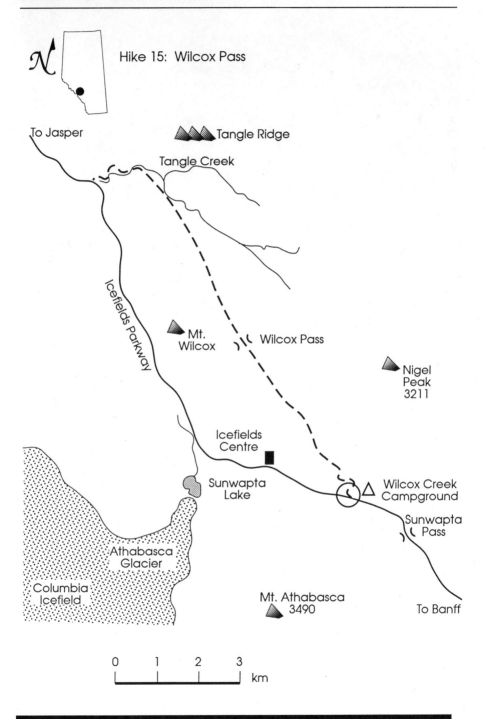

Hike 15: Wilcox Pass

To Jasper

Tangle Ridge

Tangle Creek

Icefields Parkway

Mt. Wilcox

Wilcox Pass

Nigel Peak 3211

Icefields Centre

Sunwapta Lake

Wilcox Creek Campground

Sunwapta Pass

Athabasca Glacier

Columbia Icefield

Mt. Athabasca 3490

To Banff

0   1   2   3
km

Mount Andromeda and Athabasca Glacier from Wilcox Pass.

Parkway now runs and Wilcox Pass was the route trappers and outfitters took over the Sunwapta divide. The pass can be hiked from either direction, but the southern trailhead is the more scenic approach to the pass.

The trail switchbacks steeply for roughly two kilometres through an old growth forest of subalpine firs before leveling off on a high bench overlooking the Columbia Icefield to the west. From here to the pass itself the trail meanders through alpine tundra and around meltwater ponds.

The plants and soil of this harsh climate are extremely fragile, so stay on the path and limit your cross-country travel to the numerous bighorn sheep trails. At the top of the broad pass, numerous sheep trails lead west of the main trail, providing access to 2,700 metre Mount Wilcox. The slopes of Mount Wilcox offer shelter from the winds and a panoramic view of Mount Athabasca and the Athabasca Glacier sloping away from the massive Columbia Icefield. In good weather, look for the tracks of climbing parties on the snowy faces of Mount Athabasca. Mount Wilcox also provides views of Wilcox Pass itself, where bighorn sheep, deer, grizzlies, eagles, and moose are sometimes sighted.

Many hikers simply return to the Wilcox Creek trailhead, making an eight-kilometre roundtrip. Continuing north the trail is lightly used and grows faint, following the headwaters of Tangle Creek. A marker points the way into the drainage. The most obvious track crosses the creek and hugs the flank of Tangle Ridge to the north, gaining definition as it descends into the trees. From here the trail is better defined as it drops sharply down to the Tangle Creek trailhead and parking lot, ten kilometres north of the Wilcox Creek Campground by way of the Icefields Parkway.

HIKE 16 *GERALDINE LAKES*

General description: A moderate day hike or strenuous overnight over rugged terrain to a remote lake basin.

General location: Southwest of Athabasca Falls near the middle of Jasper National Park.

Maps: Jasper National Park.

Special attractions: Two prominent waterfalls; three large lakes in the Geraldine chain; potential for solitude.

For more information: Park Superintendent, Jasper National Park, P.O. Box 10, Jasper, Alberta, TOE 1EO. Ph: (403) 852-6161.

Finding the trailhead: From the Icefields Parkway (Highway 93), turn west onto Highway 93-A at the Athabasca Falls junction. Drive north for about one kilometre and turn left onto the Geraldine access road, a rough dirt road that climbs rapidly into the forest. Follow this road six kilometres to a small parking area at the top of a series of switchbacks. The trail leaves directly from the road and is marked with a sign.

HIKE 16 *GERALDINE LAKES*

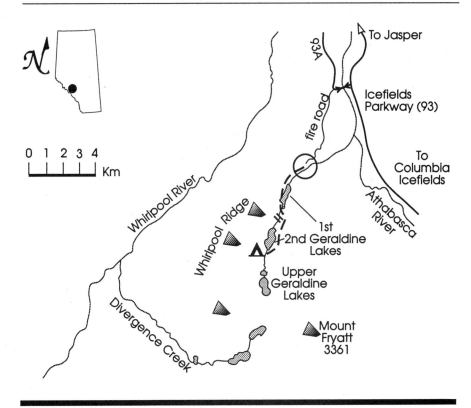

The second Geraldine Lake, looking west.

The hike: A hiking companion once described the route into the Geraldine Lakes as a miserable, root-infested, ankle-busting slog. These epithets probably tell more about the hiker than the trail, but there is some truth in them too. Hikers who venture beyond the first lake will encounter trackless boulder fields, steep scrambles up rocky headwalls, and a confusion of cairns. Bad weather intensifies the risk of a slip or losing the trail. But these same obstacles preserve the wild, remote character of the upper basin, and the alpine ridges above the upper two lakes offer some of the best terrain in the park for wandering and exploring. Day hikers can easily reach the second lake, but the upper basin is best explored from a basecamp set up at the designated site on the south end of the second lake.

The first two kilometres of trail to the lowermost lake are wet and spongy, tangled with tree roots and decaying log corduroy. This section of trail climbs gradually through a dense forest before dropping over the last 200 metres to the outlet stream and the first lake. The trail hugs the northern shore, skirting a small boulder field before stair-stepping up the first headwall beside a noisy cascade.

From the top of this headwall, the trail vanishes in a maze of boulders. Watch for cairns and stay within earshot of the stream to pick up the track again as it skirts a copse of stunted trees. The trail then crosses to the left of the rock-strewn valley bottom and passes a shallow pond. After breaking through a stand of taller trees, hikers are rewarded with unobstructed views of a 100-metre waterfall streaming from the second headwall. The trail threads through more extensive boulder fields, then climbs up the loose scree of an avalanche gully to gain the level of the second basin.

At six kilometres from the trailhead, a low ridge atop the headwall provides good views of Mount Fryatt to the southeast and Whirlpool Peak to the north. From here the track is better defined as it drops to the second lake and contours for another kilometre around the east shore to the backcountry campsite.

Overnighters will want to pack lightly because of the boulder hopping and punishing climbs up the two headwalls. Wear sturdy shoes and bring a compass and topo map for reconnoitering the basin above. A third large lake lies beyond the campsite, best reached by parallelling the stream bed south. It's also possible to traverse to the top of the open pass at the head of the Geraldine basin for a look into the headwater lakes of Divergence Creek directly south.

HIKE 17   *MOUNT EDITH CAVELL MEADOWS*

General description: A moderate day hike to high alpine meadows overlooking Mount Edith Cavell and Angel Glacier.

General location: Twenty-seven kilometres south of Jasper in Jasper National Park.

Maps: Jasper National Park.

Special attractions: Outstanding close-up views of Mount Edith Cavell and Angel Glacier; a firsthand look at the plants of the alpine zone.

For more information: Park Superintendent, Jasper National Park, P.O. Box 10, Jasper, Alberta, TOE 1EO. Ph: (403) 852-6161.

Finding the trailhead: From Jasper, drive eight kilometres south on the Icefields Parkway to the junction with 93-A. Follow 93-A south for another five kilometres to the Edith Cavell Road on the right. Drive fifteen kilometres to the end of this narrow, winding road and park in the lot below the Path of the Glacier interpretive trail. The trail to the Edith Cavell meadows begins at a stone staircase near the southeast end of the parking lot.

The hike: Mount Edith Cavell is named for a British nurse who helped allied soldiers escape occupied Belgium during World War I. For this, the Germans executed her in October of 1917. Today, each August, a memorial service is held to commemorate the anniversary of her arrest. The 3,368-metre mountain is a fitting monument to this woman's life, a singular peak that shines brightly in the sun but a somber place too, frequently veiled by clouds and reverberating with the thunder of ice and rock falls.

The eight-kilometre hike through Cavell Meadows provides a unique view of the mountain and a lesson in the harsh lives of plants that inhabit the

HIKE 17 *MOUNT EDITH CAVELL LOOP*

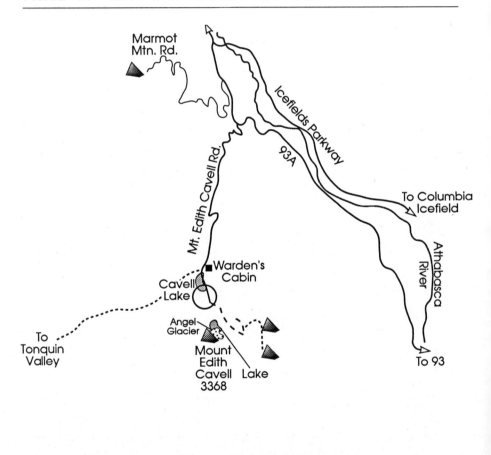

subalpine and alpine zones. Climb the staircase onto the low moraine above the parking lot and follow the paved interpretive trail southeast along a barren lateral moraine. Mount Edith Cavell dominates the view. To the right lies the scoured valley left by Angel Glacier as it receded to its present position on the lap of Mount Edith Cavell. Half a kilometre from the trailhead, a dirt track splits to the left from the paved trail (which continues straight to the shore of a small tarn at the base of Angel Glacier) and climbs onto the rocky lateral moraine. This trail winds back toward the parking lot, gaining elevation, then swings over the spine of the moraine and cuts south

Angel Glacier on Mount Edith Cavell.

between the moraine and the subalpine forest.

Soon the trail begins a moderate climb, switchbacking through the forest with occasional glimpses of the cirque and glacier. The grade eases somewhat as the trail breaks above timberline, and a viewpoint offers a good spot to rest. From here, Angel Glacier seems an arm's length away, clinging to the sheer wall of the mountain in a suspended tumble of crevasses and icefalls.

The vistas widen to include the entire northeast face of the mountain as the trail climbs higher into the alpine meadows. At four kilometres the main trail circles back to rejoin itself at timberline. A less-defined track continues up the rocky ridge to the east, offering views to the Whirlpool River below and east to the Athabasca Valley. If you do venture beyond the official trail, keep to established paths and avoid disturbing the delicate plants and fragile soil. Consider wearing running shoes or other footwear with less rugged soles on this trail to help reduce the damage done by the sheer numbers of visitors.

HIKE 18 *TONQUIN VALLEY*

General description: A moderate three- or four-day backpack to a spectacular wilderness lake beneath the crags and spires of the Continental Divide.
General location: Southwest of Jasper in Jasper National Park.
Maps: Jasper National Park; 83 D/9, 83 D/16.
Special attractions: Splendid alpine scenery, Amethyst Lakes, wildlife (including mountain caribou and grizzly bear), wildflowers, excellent backcountry day-hiking.
For more information: Park Superintendent, Jasper National Park, P.O. Box 10, Jasper, Alberta, TOE 1EO. Ph: (403) 852-6161.
Finding the trailhead: From Jasper, drive eight kilometres south on the Icefields Parkway to the junction with 93-A. Follow 93-A south for another five kilometres to the Edith Cavell Road on the right. Drive twelve kilometres on this narrow, winding road and park in the roadside area on the right. A short trail drops to the outlet of Cavell Lake, where the Astoria River trail begins.

The hike: The Tonquin Valley is one of the most stunning—and hence most popular—regions in the Canadian Rockies. This high, broad basin contains nearly every alpine feature—shimmering lakes, sawtoothed peaks capped by glaciers, windswept passes painted with wildflowers, and abundant wildlife. The Tonquin also has a reputation among hikers for its mobbed campgrounds, trails whipped to mud by pack horses, and days of rain. Because the high mountains here rake moisture from every passing weather front, the valley receives twice as much rain as Jasper townsite, only twenty kilometres to the north. Park maintenance crews can't change the climate, but they have worked diligently to upgrade seven of the valley's campgrounds and twenty kilometres of trail, "hardening" these areas to withstand continued heavy use.

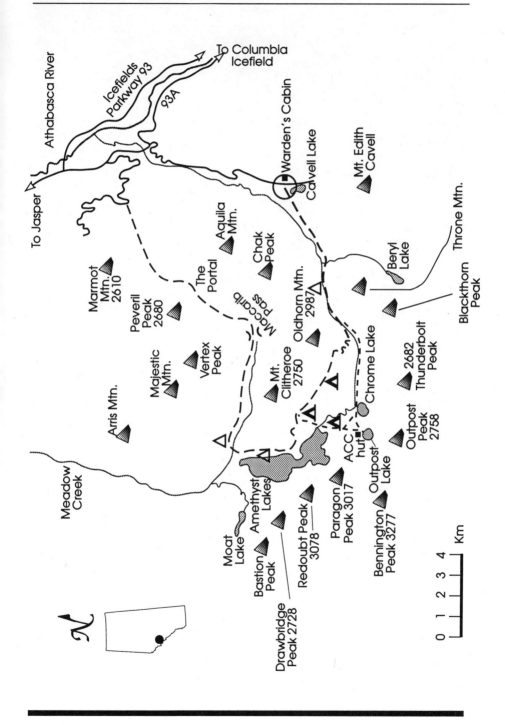

Looking west along the Astoria River Valley toward Tonquin Valley.

If you can, plan your trip to the Tonquin for the early fall. The weather is drier from late August through September, though snow is not uncommon this time of year. There are also fewer hikers on the trail, and wildlife is more visible.

From the Mount Edith Cavell Road, the trail drops gradually along the north flank of Mount Edith Cavell into the Astoria River valley. Five kilometres in, a bridge crosses to the river's north bank and begins a gentle climb. The trail passes the Astoria River Campground two kilometres after crossing the river, then forks in another kilometre. The left fork is a rough old trail to the Eremite Valley, while the main trail continues up the right fork, switchbacking madly around the base of Oldhorn Mountain. As the trail levels off, Amethyst Lakes and The Ramparts swing into view.

The 1,000-metre face of The Ramparts is aptly christened, a crenellated wall of rock and ice along the Continental Divide with individual peaks named Parapet, Dungeon, Redoubt, Turret, and Bastion. Amethyst Lakes curve around the base of these towers like a moat, and indeed there is a Moat Lake at the northwest end of the valley.

The trail passes Switchback Campground then descends to a junction with the trail to Surprise Point some seventeen kilometres from the trailhead. The two most popular campgrounds are to the left: Clitheroe just 100 metres downtrail, and Surprise Point two kilometres distant. To the right, the trail leads down to Amethyst Lakes Lodge and campground. The lodge area is best avoided by hikers seeking a wilderness experience, but Amethyst Lakes Campground—on the east shore three kilometres from the trail junction—is a pleasant alternative to Surprise Point and Clitheroe.

Perhaps the main attraction of the Tonquin Valley is the number of day-hiking options available. From a base camp at any one of the above camp-grounds, hikers can readily explore the Eremite Valley and Arrowhead Lake to the south, the shores of Amethyst Lakes, or Moat Lake and Tonquin Pass to the northwest. Plan at least two nights encamped near Amethyst Lakes.

To complete the loop, follow the Maccarib Pass trail along the east shore of Amethyst Lakes to the junction at the north end of the north lake. Turn right and begin the gradual climb up the Maccarib Creek drainage. The trail crosses the creek at Maccarib Creek Campground, one kilometre from the previous junction. From here the trail climbs steadily to the 2,210-metre pass; turn around frequently for fine views of The Ramparts and Amethyst Lakes.

From the pass, the trail drops steeply and angles north along the head of Portal Creek, climbing briefly above the creek on the base of Peveril Peak, then crossing Circus Creek and descending steadily through the subalpine forest in Portal Creek Canyon. A bridge crosses the creek 500 metres from the trailhead and parking lot on the Marmot Mountain Road. This road is practically untravelled in summer except for access to the Portal Creek trailhead, so it's best to leave a car at the trailhead before driving to the Astoria River trail. Total distance for the Astoria River-Maccarib Pass loop is forty-three kilometres.

HIKE 19   *VALLEY OF THE FIVE LAKES*

General description: An easy five kilometre half-day hike through rolling, lake-studded terrain.

General location: Nine kilometres south of the Jasper townsite along the Icefields Parkway.

Maps: Jasper 83 D/16.

Special attractions: Five emerald ponds, good fishing, and brief views of the Athabasca Valley and Mount Edith Cavell.

For more information: Park Superintendent, P.O. Box 10, Jasper, Alberta, TOE 1EO. Ph: (403) 852-6161.

HIKE 19 *VALLEY OF THE FIVE LAKES*

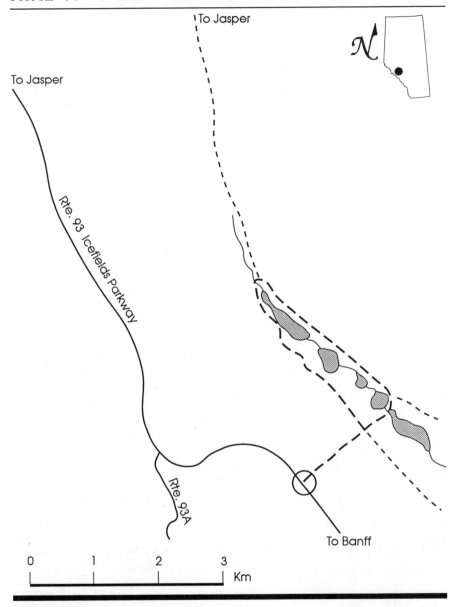

Finding the trailhead: The trailhead is well marked, about nine kilometres south of Jasper on the Icefields Parkway on the east side of the road.

The hike: Set aside two to three hours for this stroll through the Valley of the Five Lakes, or spend a day fishing for brook and rainbow trout at each of the lakes. If you plan to fish, purchase a Jasper National Park fishing license at the park office or a sporting goods store in Jasper. The solid trail and rolling terrain make this a great hike for leaving the boots in the car and lacing up a comfortable pair of tennis shoes. You might want to bring along a bathing suit if the day is hot.

The first kilometre of trail cuts across the forested flats of the Athabasca River Valley and climbs a small ridge, providing fine views of the valley and 3,363 metre Mount Edith Cavell to the west. Then the trail drops into the Valley of the Five Lakes and joins a major hiking route between Jasper and the Maligne mountains.

For an enjoyable loop hike, turn left and walk to another trail junction at the northern end of the northernmost and largest lake. Turn right and follow this trail south along the eastern shoreline of the lakes. A variety of wildlife frequents this drainage. Watch for signs of beaver, elk, deer, coyote, and bear along the way. You will also revel in the wildflower displays early in the year.

The southbound trail leads to each lake and then branches to the west just above the last lake, finally connecting with the path back to the trailhead.

One of the lakes in the Valley of the Five Lakes.

HIKE 20 *THE WHISTLERS*

General description: A ride on an aerial tram and an easy day hike to the panoramic summit of The Whistlers.

General location: Immediately southwest of the Jasper townsite in Jasper National Park.

Maps: Jasper National Park; Jasper 83 D/16.

Special attractions: A ride on the longest aerial tram in Canada, panoramic views from atop a high alpine summit, pikas, marmots, occasional birds of prey.

For more information: Park Superintendent, Jasper National Park, P.O. Box 10, Jasper, Alberta, TOE 1EO. Ph: (403) 852-6161.

Finding the trailhead: From Jasper townsite, drive south on the Icefields Parkway (93) for two kilometres to the Whistlers Road. Turn right and drive four kilometres to the parking lot and lower tram terminal at the end of the road.

The hike: The Whistlers is a broad, barren 2,470-metre summit that looms over the town of Jasper and the confluence of the Miette and Athabasca valleys. The peak's name honors the hoary marmots that live among the

The lower tram station on Whistlers.

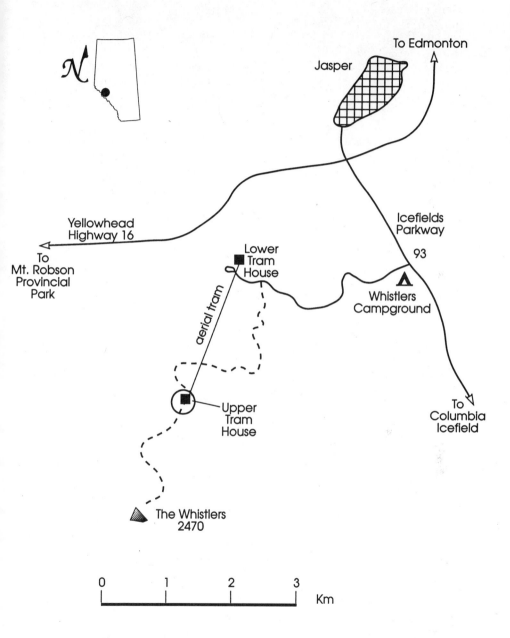

summit boulder fields, whistling their warning cry through the colony whenever danger approaches. The trail running along the summit ridge offers one of the finest opportunities for families and casual hikers to visit the alpine world and to see many of Jasper's glacier-carved crags in a single sweep of the horizon. Even experienced alpinists will enjoy the spectacular vistas—and an option to roam the high country beyond the end of the trail.

The Whistlers environment is harsh—usually windy and cold even in mid-summer. Pack a sweater and windproof coat, a warm hat that won't blow off, and sunglasses. Don't forget the camera and binoculars. For those planning to explore beyond the summit, wear sturdy boots and carry lunch and plenty of water. Bear in mind that alpine plants and soil are extremely fragile; don't step on or pick flowers, and refrain from overturning rocks. Stay on established trails, and beyond trail's end tread lightly.

A few hardy souls hike the Whistlers from the base of the mountain, beginning at the trailhead on the Whistlers Road one kilometre below the lower tram terminal. This route traverses three ecological zones as it climbs over 1,200 metres in eight kilometres. The ascent is steep, sweaty work, crossing twice beneath the tram lines before joining the summit trail at the upper tram terminal.

Most hikers opt to glide over the lower slopes on the Jasper Tramway, which covers a 1,100-metre elevation gain in just over seven minutes. The tram is the longest aerial cablecar in Canada, spanning 2,000 metres between the lower and upper terminals. As of this writing, the roundtrip fee is $9 per adult, children ages five through twelve years ride for half-price, and children under five go for free.

From the upper terminal, the wide, well-defined trail climbs directly up the nose of a prominent ridge toward the summit. One pitch is particularly steep, but a spur trail to the left contours around this knob, revealing excellent views of the Athabasca River and the distant Maligne Range to the southeast. The trail winds south and rises quickly to the summit, roughly 1.5 kilometres from the upper terminal. Stop at the 360-degree sighting dial to line up the brass pointer with the many peaks ringing the horizon. The Trident Range, close at hand to the southwest, features Terminal Mountain, Vertex Peak, Peveril Peak, and Manx Peak.

Though most hikers return to the tram terminal after a brief rest at the summit, avid trekkers may continue beyond the end of the trail, dropping into the open saddle southwest from the summit to ascend the southeast arm of Indian Ridge. A string of rock cairns points the way from The Whistlers, but the track soon scatters. Stay on the highest contour available; you may find a trace as the climb up Indian Ridge narrows along the ridge top. Views from the ridge include Muhigan Peak to the northwest, Indian Pass, and an eagle-eye look at the meanders and meadows of Whistlers Creek to the south. Remember to allow time for the return trip to the upper tram terminal to catch the last run of the day, or follow the footpath around the west side of the terminal and walk the seven kilometres down to the trailhead.

HIKE 21 *SATURDAY NIGHT LAKE LOOP*

General description: An easy overnight loop to a number of forest-rimmed lakes, starting and ending in downtown Jasper.

General location: West of the Jasper townsite in Jasper National Park.

Maps: Jasper National Park; Jasper 83 D/16.

Special attractions: More than half a dozen lakes, good fishing, and bountiful wildflowers.

For more information: Park Superintendent, Jasper National Park, P.O. Box 10, Jasper, Alberta, TOE 1EO. Ph: (403) 852-6161.

Finding the trailhead: Several trailheads on the west edge of the Jasper townsite connect with the Saturday Night Lake loop. The best of these is found at the southwest corner of town, near the mobile home park. From Jasper's main street, Connaught Drive, turn west on Cedar Avenue, which then becomes Pyramid Avenue. At the edge of town, turn left on Pyramid Lake Drive and then right on Cabin Creek Road. Stay on Cabin Creek for 1.5 kilometres, veering right at every road junction. Just opposite the mobile home park, a gravel road takes off uphill to the parking lot and trail sign fifty metres on the left.

The hike: This twenty-five kilometre loop on the heavily timbered Pyramid Plateau just west of the Jasper townsite is an excellent choice for casual backpackers and families. The trail gains only 640 metres in elevation over its length, reaching a high point of 1,700 metres near Minnow Lake. The drawback is that hikers never break above timberline and views are limited. But the forest offers its own rewards: a handful of small, serene lakes full of trout; primitive but sheltered and quiet campsites at three of the lakes; and an abundance of interesting wildflowers along the path.

The trail crosses Cabin Creek and climbs onto the plateau proper, skirting Marjorie Lake on the left. From the far end of the lake, a short side trail to the right leads to Hibernia Lake one kilometre distant. The main trail continues on to Caledonia Lake, again to the left of the trail.

Look for wildflowers, particularly in the open areas near each lake. Lilies and roses mingle with arnica, paintbrush, Labrador tea, lupine, and calypso orchids. Also watch for dark-eyed juncoes, grey jays, the ever present raven, and osprey fishing the lakes. Moose are sometimes seen, and black bears occasionally visit careless campers—keep a clean camp and hang your food.

Camping along this loop is in designated sites only. The first of these is found at Minnow Lake, less than one kilometre northwest of the main trail. From the Minnow Lake junction, the main trail climbs three kilometres to another junction with the side trail to High Lakes and another campsite about 200 metres to the right.

Just beyond High Lakes, the trail passes the foot of a tumbling waterfall and the remainder of the loop gradually descends past bogs and swamps. Roughly eighteen kilometres from the start and seven kilometres from the

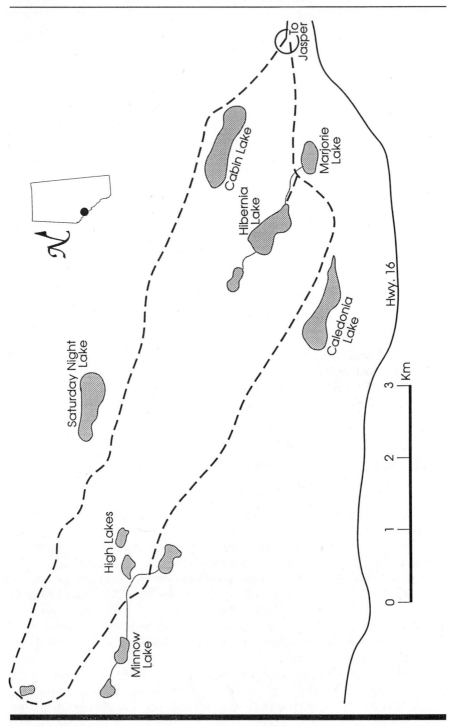

end of the hike, another side trail to the left climbs 500 metres to Saturday Night Lake, and the third designated campsite on the loop.

From the Saturday Night Lake junction, follow the main trail down to Cabin Lake, Jasper's source of drinking water and the only lake on the loop where fishing is not allowed. Cross the earthen dam at the east end of Cabin Lake and walk down the access road, crossing the stream on a footbridge to the left. The trail opens onto a bluff above the Athabasca Valley and then drops through the trees back to the trailhead.

HIKE 22 *JACQUES LAKE*

General description: A three-day backpack on a little-used trail to the timbered shores of Jacques Lake.
General location: Fifteen kilometres northeast of Jasper in Jasper National Park.
Maps: Jasper National Park; 83 C/13.
Special attractions: Good prospects for solitude, a string of forested lakes, wildlife.
For more information: Park Superintendent, Jasper National Park, P.O. Box 10, Jasper, Alberta, TOE 1EO. Ph: (403) 852-6161.
Finding the trailhead: From Jasper, drive twenty-three kilometres north on the Yellowhead Highway (16) to the trailhead parking area on the east side of the road. Look for this parking lot about three kilometres past the highway bridge over the Athabasca River. The trail begins at the east end of the parking lot, leading into the brushy outwash plain of Jacques Creek.

The hike: Veteran hikers can sometimes be overheard grumbling about crowded trails and the paucity of solitude in Alberta's mountain parks. During the peak of the hiking season, these complaints often ring true on all but a few forgotten trails. The hike to Jacques Lake follows such a trail, wandering the quiet, unpopulated corridor between the limestone ribs of the Jacques Range and Colin Ridge. In places, this track is ill-defined and poorly maintained—sure signs of scant traffic. Carry a topo map and compass to aid in route-finding, and be prepared for a handful of unbridged stream crossings.

After the first kilometre through the open brush, the trail enters the densely forested Jacques Creek drainage, crossing the creek several times as it climbs steadily to 1,800-metre Jacques Pass. Emir Campground lies .5 kilometre below the pass, about eleven kilometres from the trailhead, and Nashan Campground is found just four kilometres down the east slope of the pass near Nashan Creek. Of these two campgrounds, Nashan is the more remote and is exactly midway between the trailhead and Jacques Lake.

After crossing Nashan Creek, the trail climbs dauntingly for four kilometres to 1,930-metre Merlin Pass, a narrow passage below Mount Merlin to the north. The trail then drops sharply to Dromore Creek and campground, skirting the north side of the creek and bending with it to the east before crossing the stream below Sirdar Mountain. From here the trail climbs steeply again for three kilometres to a broad, wooded pass just under 1,800 metres. The junction with the Jacques Lake Trail is reached in another four kilometres; turn left for the campground at the lake's outlet, one kilometre from the junction and thirty kilometres from the trailhead on the Yellowhead Highway.

Jacques Lake is surrounded by lush forest with open views of the Queen Elizabeth Range to the southeast. A warden's cabin sits below the lake, just downstream from where the trail crosses the outlet.

To exit the Jacques Lake basin, hike back to the Merlin Pass trail junction

HIKE 22 *JACQUES LAKE*

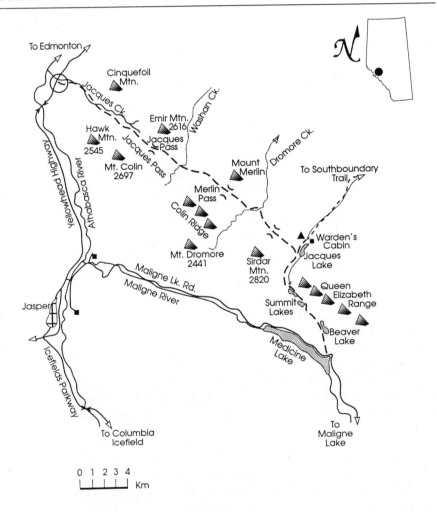

and bear straight ahead on the Jacques Lake trail. This route is more heavily travelled, providing access for day hikers from the Maligne Lake Road some twelve kilometres away.

The trail climbs alongside a feeder stream, crossing it and several side streams many times. Shortly, the trail angles to the left, crosses the main stream once again, and skirts Summit Lakes, a string of limestone sinks. Here the trail joins an old fire road and descends gradually to the serene shores of Beaver Lake, the largest lake on this circuit. Find a lakeshore log for a final look at the Queen Elizabeth Range and perhaps a glimpse of teal or loon. The trailhead, at the Beaver Creek picnic area, is two easy kilometres downtrail.

It's best to leave a car at the Beaver Creek picnic area (twenty-eight kilometres on the Maligne Lake Road from the Yellowhead Highway) before driving to the Merlin Pass trailhead. Traffic on the Maligne Lake Road can be sparse late in the day, and hitchhiking has become less certain in recent years.

Beaver Lake and the Queen Elizabeth Range.

65

HIKE 23 *MONA LAKE LOOP*

General description: An easy half-day hike to a pair of forest lakes in the hills above Maligne Lake.

General location: East of the outlet of Maligne Lake in Jasper National Park.

Maps: Jasper National Park; 83 C/12.

Special attractions: Views of spectacular Maligne Lake at the trailhead, Lorraine and Mona lakes, moose and elk.

For more information: Park Superintendent, Jasper National Park, P.O. Box 10, Jasper, Alberta, TOE 1EO. Ph: (403) 852-6161.

Finding the trailhead: From Jasper, drive five kilometres east on the Yellowhead Highway (16) to the Maligne Lake Road. Drive south for forty-five kilometres, past the tour boat concession and restaurant, to the parking lot at the end of the road just across the bridge over the outlet. The trail begins near the lower end of the parking lot on the west side (do not confuse this trailhead with the gated fire road at the head of the parking lot).

Mona Lake, a pleasant resting spot for waterfowl and hikers alike.

The hike: Mona and Lorraine lakes are placid antidotes to the breath-taking prospect of Maligne Lake (pronounced "Muh-LEEN") and its ice-bound pinnacles. A deep mixed conifer forest encircles both lakes, revealing only a distant spire or snowy ridge through the tree tops. The trail is gentle, nearly flat, and easy to follow. As a route to the Bald Hills to the west, the path is more popular than the lakes themselves, but the trail is rarely busy.

The trail immediately enters the trees above the road and climbs gradually to a bench above the Maligne River drainage. A horse trail joins the main track about 200 metres from the trailhead; bear left at this junction. From here

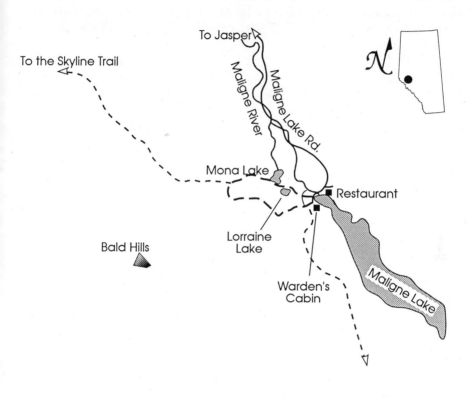

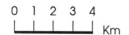

To Jasper

To the Skyline Trail

Maligne River

Maligne Lake Rd.

Mona Lake

Restaurant

Lorraine
Lake

Bald Hills

Warden's
Cabin

Maligne Lake

0 1 2 3 4
Km

the path winds through the trees, rolling over low hillocks and down into damp swales. Just under two kilometres from the trailhead a side trail breaks to the left to Lorraine Lake. This spur skirts a shallow pond and then hops over a wooded rise to the shore of Lorraine Lake.

Continue on the main trail west for another 800 metres to a second side trail, this one to the right. This spur leads quickly down to the south end of Mona Lake, a wide, shallow kettle favoured by waterfowl. A faint track leads around the east shore, but if other hikers are scarce the south end offers a fine lunch spot overlooking the lake.

Rather than backtrack to the trailhead, hikers can proceed west from Mona Lake to the junction with an old fire road. Turn left for an easy five-kilometre stroll back to the parking lot above Maligne Lake.

Front Range

HIKE 24 *CADOMIN CAVES*

General description: A moderate half-day hike to one of the largest limestone caverns yet discovered in the Canadian Rockies.
General location: In the mountains east of Jasper National Park in west central Alberta.
Maps: 83 F/3.
Special attractions: Cadomin Caves, rugged mountain scenery, wildlife.
For more information: Edson Forest, Bag 9000, Edson, Alberta, TOE OPO. Ph: (403) 723-3391.
Finding the trailhead: The trailhead to Cadomin Caves is well off the beaten track. From Edmonton, drive west on the Yellowhead Highway (16) to the town of Edson. Continue west on Highway 16 another ten kilometres and turn south on Highway 47. Drive ninety-six kilometres to the former mining town of Cadomin. Bear south through Cadomin on Highway 47 and watch for a graded parking lot on the left about two kilometres from town.

The hike: Although the Cadomin Caves are the main attraction on this hike, the mountain scenery and opportunities for viewing wildlife make this an enjoyable day hike even for those with no inclination to go underground. All hiking parties are encouraged to take a flashlight along, for a taste of spelunking at the entrance chamber before continuing on to the overlook above the McLeod River.

The trail begins as a jeep track on the right (west) side of the road about 100 metres back toward Cadomin from the parking lot. This two-track climbs into an increasingly narrow valley, where it becomes a well-defined trail. After 2.5 kilometres, the trail crosses the creek bed, which is usually dry except in spring and early summer. After crossing the creek, the trail makes a hairpin turn to the left. Twenty-five metres beyond the turn, the path to the caves branches to the right and begins a steady, steep climb through stunted fir and across an open slope. Follow the trail to the cave entrance at the base of massive limestone cliffs that form the front of the mountain range. The cave entrance lies roughly three kilometres from the trailhead.

Hikers with caving skills and equipment can venture through the entrance into a labyrinth of halls and chambers stretching over 1,700 metres.

HIKE 24 *CADOMIN CAVES*

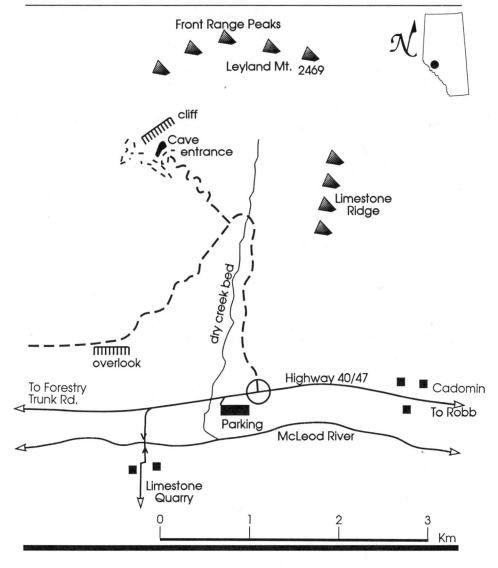

Only experienced spelunkers should enter Cadomin Caves, taking a minimum of two flashlights, extra batteries, protective clothing, gloves, and a hard hat. Many side passages branch off of the main gallery, and cave explorers should mark a return route with rock cairns or fishing line. A detailed map of the cave system is available at the general store in Cadomin.

Hikers who prefer to stay above ground can return to the main trail and continue along it to the southeast. The gradient is gentle and the trail leads to a terrace overlooking the McLeod River Valley with magnificent mountain views in all directions. A spur trail continues up the steep bedrock ridge above the terrace to a higher vantage point.

Retrace the main trail to return to the trailhead, allowing four to five hours for the round trip. —*Peter Allen*

The trail up the narrowing valley to Cadomin Caves. Peter Allen photo

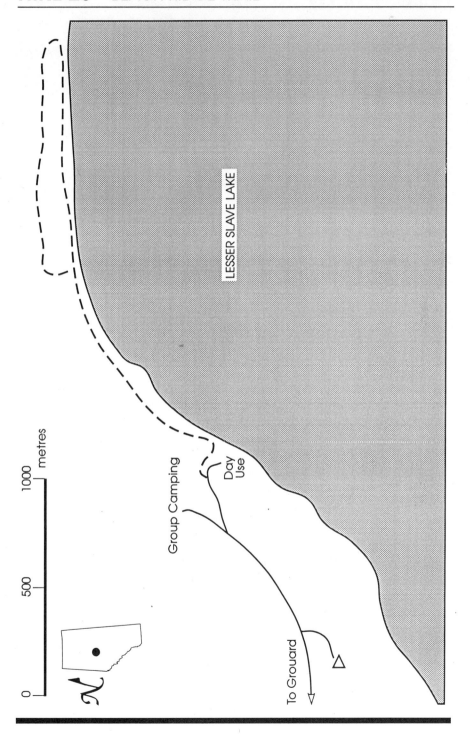

LESSER SLAVE LAKE

Group Camping

Day Use

To Grouard

metres

0   500   1000

N

Hilliard's Bay Provincial Park

HIKE 25 BEACH RIDGE TRAIL

General description: An easy stroll above the northern shore of Lesser Slave Lake.

General location: On the northwest corner of Lesser Slave Lake in Hilliard's Bay Provincial Park.

Maps: 83 N/9; park Winter Fun brochure.

Special attractions: Beautiful views of the lake, chances to see moose, deer, waterfowl.

For more information: Hilliard's Bay Provincial Park, General Delivery, Grouard, Alberta, TOG 1CO. Ph: (403) 751-3789.

Finding the trailhead: To reach Hilliard's Bay Provincial Park, turn north onto Route 750 from Highway 2 about seventeen kilometres west of the town of High Prairie. Drive eighteen kilometres, continue past the town of Grouard and turn east for another seven kilometres to the park. The trailhead is found at the day-use area, four kilometres from the park entrance and office, between the parking lot and the beach.

The hike: This six-kilometre hike offers excellent views of Lesser Slave Lake, the second largest lake in Alberta, and a more intimate look at the boreal forest. Take an hour or two to stretch your legs on this remote trail.

From the day-use area, the trail angles north and east along the lakeshore for roughly 2.5 kilometres, crossing several streams and ravines on footbridges. Watch for deer and moose tracks crossing the trail through the aspen forest, which is layered with cranberry, wild rose, and other wildflowers. The forest is also home to an array of birds, including spruce grouse, chickadees, woodpeckers, great-horned owls, warblers, and many other songbirds.

On the return loop, the trail climbs gradually into a mixed boreal forest, offering excellent views of the lake. Keep an eye out for bald eagles, osprey, loons, and pelicans along the lakeshore. The trail then drops steeply, joining the main trail just over one kilometre from the trailhead.

Hilliard's Bay offers a large campground, playgrounds, a boat ramp, picnic shelters, and interpretive programs at the campground ampitheatre. Lesser Slave Lake boasts excellent walleye, perch, and northern pike fishing, and park beaches provide good swimming. —*Carter Cox*

Lesser Slave Lake Provincial Park

HIKE 26 *LILY LAKE*

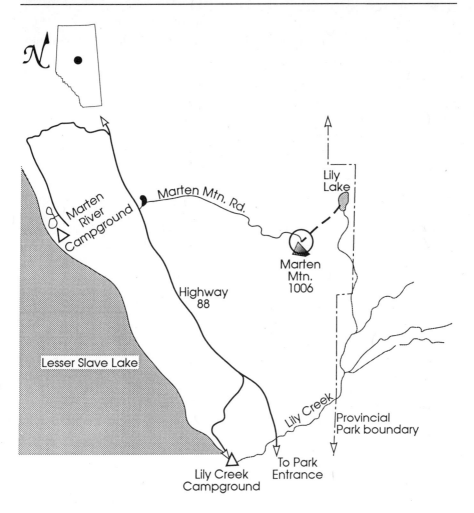

HIKE 26 *LILY LAKE*

General description: A moderate day hike through old growth forest to a small lake with good fishing.

General location: On the east shore of Lesser Slave Lake, 250 kilometres north of Edmonton.

Maps: 83 O/7; Marten River Campground Guide brochure.

Special attractions: Views from Marten Mountain, secluded Lily Lake, good fishing for brook trout, old growth forest, wildlife.

For more information: Lesser Slave Lake Provincial Park, Box 730, Slave Lake, Alberta, TOG 2AO. Ph: (403) 849-7100.

Finding the trailhead: Follow Route 88 north for twenty-one kilometres from the town of Slave Lake to the park boundary. Two and one-half kilometres north of the park entrance, look for a sign for the Marten Mountain viewpoint and turn right onto the Marten Mountain access road. This six-kilometre road climbs and winds its way to the summit of Marten Mountain, where there is a parking lot, picnic area, and viewpoint. The trailhead is marked with a sign and map on the road just east of the parking lot.

The hike: The trail to Lily Lake is one of the more interesting short hikes in northern Alberta. The rough, rolling path cuts through an old growth forest of balsam fir and lodgepole pine, dropping a total of 185 metres in elevation from the summit of 1,006-metre Marten Mountain to the shores of Lily Lake. This area straddles the line where species of the Great Plains meet the denizens of the boreal forest, and the slopes of Marten Mountain also play host to species more commonly found in the western foothills.

Watch for the Cape May and bay-breasted warbler in the woods, loons and waterfowl at Lily Lake, and six different species of woodpecker. Also found here are moose, white-tailed deer, marten, fisher, lynx, and black bear. In recent years, a female grizzly has been sighted near Lily Lake, and a bear den (probably black bear) can be found at the north end of the lake. At the south end, an old beaver dam curves across the outlet stream. Lily Lake is stocked with eastern brook trout and the fishing is good.

The trail was built in 1975 and still awaits finishing touches; wear sturdy boots and be prepared for standing water in lower sections of the trail. Plans call for steps to be installed on several steep pitches, but as of this writing hikers must scramble up and boot ski down these grades. Also be aware that overnight camping is prohibited at Lily Lake.

The trail dips and climbs frequently, crossing four stream beds in three kilometres before reaching a small picnic spot on the southwest end of Lily Lake. Along the way there's five-leaf trailing raspberry, heartleaf arnica, and stands of western ash. Beware the spines of devil's club, an uncommon plant in these parts, which can cause severe irritation to the skin. Take a fishing pole along (and your provincial fishing license) for a change of pace from the perch, walleye, and northern pike fishing at Lesser Slave Lake.—*Frank Fraser*

Wood Buffalo National Park

Straddling Alberta's border with the Northwest Territories, Wood Buffalo covers nearly 45,000 square kilometres of remote boreal forest, salt plains, muskegs, river delta, and prairie. It is one of the largest national parks in the world, nesting ground for the rare whooping crane, and home to 2,800 free-roaming bison. Any trip north to this remote park warrants a minimum of a week stay, and a lifetime would be insufficient for exploring every corner of the park.

Travellers arriving at Wood Buffalo will find hotel accommodations at Fort Smith and Fort Chipewyan. Campgrounds are located in Fort Smith within the park and at Pine Lake. Road conditions vary with the weather and most park roads are open during summer only. The hiking season runs from May through September, though bad weather or flooding may limit backcountry access at any time. Be prepared for insects, wet footing, and temperature extremes. Hikers must be self-reliant and able to cope with wilderness route-finding, first-aid emergencies, and isolation.

Before planning a trip to Wood Buffalo, contact the park staff for up-to-date information and answers to any specific queries you might have. Write to the Park Superintendent, Wood Buffalo National Park, Box 750, Fort Smith, Northwest Territories, XOE OPO.

HIKE 27 *RAINBOW LAKES*

General description: A moderate day hike or overnight through a rugged landscape of caves, sinkholes, and other geological features.
General location: North of the Parson's Lake Road in the northeast corner of Wood Buffalo National Park.
Maps: 84 P.
Special attractions: Karst landscape, bison, wildflowers, and Rainbow Lakes.
For more information: Park Superintendent, Wood Buffalo National Park, Box 750, Fort Smith, Northwest Territories, XOE OPO. Ph: (403) 872-2349 or Park office, Box 38, Fort Chipewyan, Alberta, TOP 1BO. Ph: (403) 697-3662.
Finding the trailhead: To reach the trailhead, drive approximately forty kilometres south from Fort Smith on the main park road. Turn right on the Parson's Lake Road and continue another six kilometres to the trailhead sign. It is best to leave a second vehicle at the northern Rainbow Lakes trailhead on the main park road about eight kilometres south of the Salt River crossing, or arrange to have someone pick you up there at the end of your hike.

The hike: Wood Buffalo is Canada's largest national park, a northern wilderness of mighty rivers, boreal forests, grassy meadows, and vast wetlands. The park is sanctuary to the endangered whooping crane and the largest free-roaming bison herd in the world.

Summer days are warm and typically sunny, but mosquitoes and biting flies abound from June through August. Bug jackets and repellent are essential. Wood Buffalo National Park is renowned for its profusion of wildlife, but this wilderness park also boasts the most extensive gypsum karst terrain in the world. "Karst" is a landscape of sinkholes, caves, and underground channels formed by water as it dissolves limestone or gypsum bedrock. The trail to Rainbow Lakes leads to a number of interesting karst features, including the lakes themselves.

From the Parson's Lake Road, the trail heads north along a level bison path through a forest of jackpine, entering a long dry valley headed by sheer limestone cliffs. These cliffs are actually the walls of a sinkhole created when the roof of an underground cave collapsed. Beyond the cliffs, the trail crosses meadows of wildflowers in an aspen and spruce parkland. Look for three-flowered avens and prairie crocus in the meadows and pink pyrola and

---

HIKE 27 *RAINBOW LAKES*

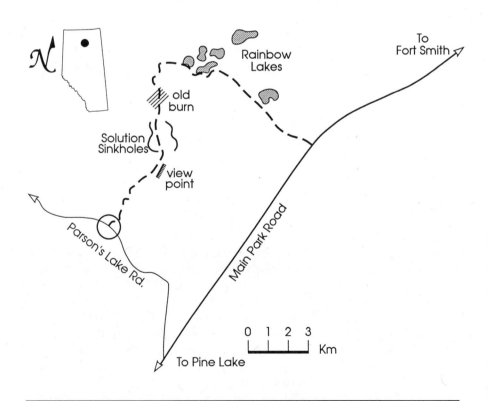

calypso orchids under the trees.

Roughly five kilometres into the hike the trail climbs a steep hill overlooking forests and meadows dotted with bison wallows. This is a good vantage point from which to look for bison and other wildlife. From here, the trail aims directly north through a mature aspen forest and an area rich in solution sinkholes, formed as water pools on the ground and dissolves the bedrock.

As you near Rainbow Lakes, the trail enters a jackpine forest with evidence of old forest fires. The lakes are as colourful as their name suggests. They are water-filled sinkholes—clear, deep, and cold, with good fishing. There are several good campsites around this scattering of lakes. Remember to pick up a backcountry permit in Fort Smith if you plan to stay overnight.

From the lakes, follow the old road or cutline the remaining six kilomteres to the parking lot at the main park road.—*Natalie Humenuk-Bourke*

HIKE 28   *SWEETGRASS STATION*

General description: A two-stage expedition in a remote wilderness for experienced canoeists and hikers.
General location: Near the north shore of Lake Claire in Wood Buffalo National Park.
Maps: 84 I (Lake Claire), 74 L (Fort Chipewyan), 84 P (Peace Point).
Special attractions: Large herds of wild bison, wolves, birds of prey, and an abundance of waterfowl and wildlife.
For more information: Park Superintendent, Wood Buffalo National Park, Box 750, Fort Smith, Northwest Territories, XOE OPO. Ph: (403) 872-2349 or Park office, Box 38, Fort Chipewyan, Alberta, TOP 1BO. Ph: (403) 697-3662.
Finding the trailhead: A trip to Sweetgrass Station begins on the Peace River. In this part of the delta, the river is big and braids into many channels. Stop at the park office in Fort Smith for maps, detailed directions, up-to-date river conditions, and a backcountry permit. A licensed park guide can be hired at Fort Chipewyan for a motorboat ride to the trailhead at Sweetgrass Landing. But if you plan to canoe the first leg, drive on the park road from Fort Smith to Peace Point and paddle downstream the sixty-six kilometres to Sweetgrass Landing—a ten- to twelve- hour paddle, possibly requiring an overnight on the river. If you don't own a canoe, one can be rented and a shuttle arranged in Fort Smith.

The hike: At 45,000-square kilometres, Wood Buffalo is Canada's largest national park. It is also extremely remote, and the park's vast backcountry offers incomparable wilderness and solitude. Backcountry travellers must be prepared for harsh weather, mosquitoes, and limited sources for good drinking water. Only experienced canoeists and hikers should attempt the trip to Sweetgrass Station.

Sweetgrass Station lies on the edge of a vast complex of meadows within the delta of the Peace and Athabasca rivers, one of the largest freshwater deltas in the world. The meadows are a favoured feeding ground for large herds of bison, and wolves also frequent the area. A visit to Sweetgrass Station offers a unique opportunity to observe the natural interaction between predators and prey in a wild setting. Lake Claire and the surround-

HIKE 28 *SWEETGRASS STATION*

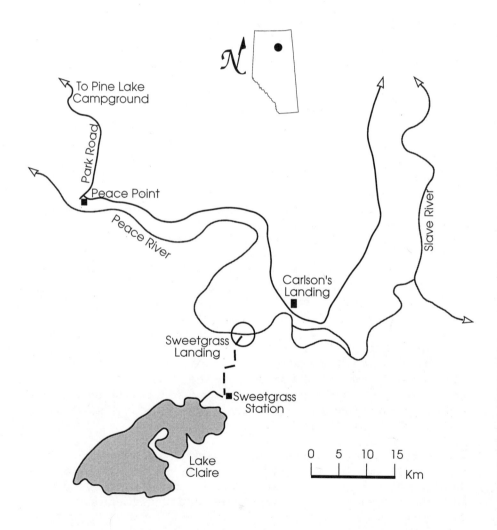

ing marshlands attract flocks of waterfowl, shorebirds, and birds of prey. Plan a minimum of three days for this Albertan safari.

Sweetgrass Landing itself is a small clearing on the south bank of the Peace River, marked by an obvious dip in the stream bank. The trailhead is posted with a sign, and there is a brown outhouse in the bush back from the river. The trail is wide, mostly level, and easy to follow, proceeding south through a mosaic of boreal forest for twelve kilometres. Bison commonly use the trail, and the trampled ground makes for rough going in some stretches and muddy footing in wet weather. About eleven kilometres into the hike, you will come across remnants of old corrals. The trail follows these corrals to the station.

A visitor cabin is available at the station, complete with six bunks and two cots, and a wood-burning cookstove. Up to twelve people can use the cabin at once. Sweetgrass Creek runs nearby and may be used for drinking water, but park officials recommend filtering the water and boiling it for ten minutes. Use of the cabin is free, but pre-registration at the park office in Fort Smith is required.

There is also ample room for tenting if you prefer to camp, though you should find a site at least 1.5 kilometres from the trail. Park officials stress the importance of using no-impact camping methods, particularly when visitor use is concentrated such as at the Sweetgrass cabin. A use permit is required for anyone planning to spend a night in the backcountry.

Careful planning and mastery of the appropriate backcountry skills will ensure a safe, unforgettable wilderness adventure in the Sweetgrass meadows.—*Natalie Humenuk-Bourke*

Whitney Lakes Provincial Park

HIKE 29   *ROSS LAKE TRAILS*

General description: Two easy strolls through the woods surrounding Ross Lake.
General location: East of Elk Lake near the Saskatchewan border.
Maps: Ross Lake Trail brochure, Whitney Lakes Provincial Park brochure.
Special attractions: Ross Lake, waterfowl, swimming, fishing, wildlife.
For more information: Whitney Lakes Provincial Park, Box 39, Elk Point, Alberta, TOA 1AO. Ph: (403) 943-3761.
Finding the trailhead: Day-use visitors can park either at the day-use area north of the park entrance or at the boat launch parking lot. From the boat launch, walk north for 200 metres and turn right at the next trail junction. From the day-use picnic area, follow the short path that begins by the water spigot to the Ross Lake trailhead.

Hikers on the Ross Lake Trail. Photo courtesy of Whitney Lakes Provincial Park.

The hike: Most visitors to Whitney Lakes Provincial Park come to fish and boat, swim, view wildlife, or just relax in one of the two campgrounds. Three of the park's lakes offer good perch and pike fishing, and boat launch ramps are provided at Ross, Whitney, and Laurier lakes. Ross Lake campground has 149 sites clustered along the south and east shores of the lake. Picnic shelters, group camping areas, beaches for swimming, showers, and firewood are available. A gravel path along the lakeshore and a self-guided interpretive trail give campers and day visitors an excuse to stretch their legs.

The first trail is an informal shoreline path that links most of the campground facilities ringing the lake from the boat launch on the west shore to the walk-in tent sites on the east shore. Campers can step onto this 2.5 kilometre trail from any of the six campsite loops.

The second trail is the Ross Lake interpretive trail, a one-kilometre loop on the northwest end of the lake. A trailhead sign with a brochure dispenser contains interpretive trail guides with descriptions of the area's ecological features corresponding to numbered posts along the way. From the trailhead, walk 150 metres and take the right-hand fork at the next junction.

The first leg of the trail winds through a mixed forest of aspen, poplar, paper birch, and white spruce. Undergrowth here is thick, as in most poplar forests. Further on, the trail enters a mature spruce forest with a ground cover of more shade-tolerant plants such as mosses and fungi.

Whitney Lakes Provincial Park spans the border between the aspen parkland ecoregion to the south and the boreal forest to the north. Plant and animal species from both ecoregions can be found here. Watch for ruffed grouse and pileated woodpeckers, beaver and black bears.

As the loop closes, the trail follows the edge of a pond frequented by red-necked grebes, goldeneyes, and other waterfowl. Interpretive brochures can be returned to the trailhead box for others to use.

HIKE 29 *ROSS LAKE TRAILS*

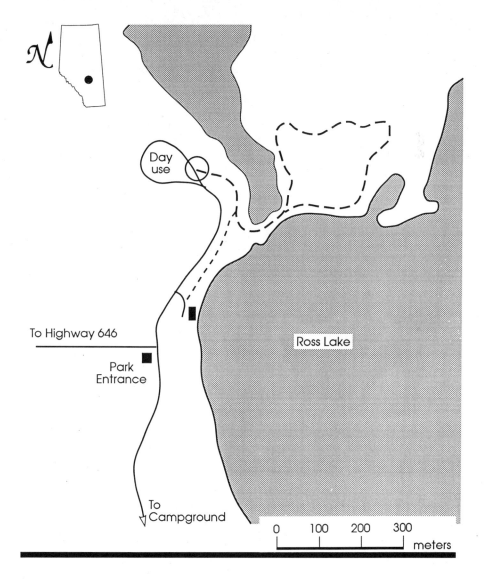

With the knowledge of local flora and fauna gained from the Ross Lake Trail, more adventurous hikers may want to strike out on the informal trail that branches north from Highway 646 into the isthmus between Whitney, Borden, and Laurier lakes. This unmarked hike offers vistas of the lakes, abundant wildlife, and a firsthand look at the eskers and other glacial landforms represented in the park. Blueberries, Saskatoon berries, and chokecherries are common along the way. Stop at the park office and ask a ranger for directions to the trailhead and current trail conditions.
—*Kerry Hope*

Vermilion Provincial Park

HIKE 30 *VERMILION LOOPS*

General description: An easy day hike through the aspen parkland along the Vermilion River.

General location: West of the town of Vermilion, sixty kilometres west of Lloydminster.

Maps: Vermilion Trail Map, park brochure.

Special attractions: Vermilion River and reservoir, wildlife, waterfowl, an interpretive brochure describing the hike.

For more information: Vermilion Provincial Park, P.O. Box 1140, Vermilion, Alberta, TOB 4MO. Ph: (403) 853-8159.

Finding the trailhead: To reach the park, drive north on Highway 41 to the town of Vermilion and turn west onto 50th Avenue, watching for provincial park signs. Turn right at the "T" intersection, and right again on the park entrance road. If you plan to camp at the park, ask for a site near one of the two spur trails leading to the Aspen Trail. These trailheads lie between campsites 23 and 24, and between sites 89 and 90. Day-use visitors should drive past the campground entrance to the beach and picnic area parking lot by the reservoir. The Aspen Trail begins on the north side of the main park road, just west of the train station.

The hike: The trail system at Vermilion Provincial Park includes ten kilometres of short loop hikes, each connected to the next. The hike outlined here covers over nine kilometres of the trail system as it parallels the shores of the Vermilion River and reservoir, traversing aspen forest, meadows, and wetlands.

The Aspen Trail threads through a dense aspen and poplar forest between the campground and the reservoir. Sunlight dapples the forest floor nourishing a lush carpet of undergrowth including wild vetch, saskatoon berry, and fairy bells.

HIKE 30 *VERMILION LOOPS*

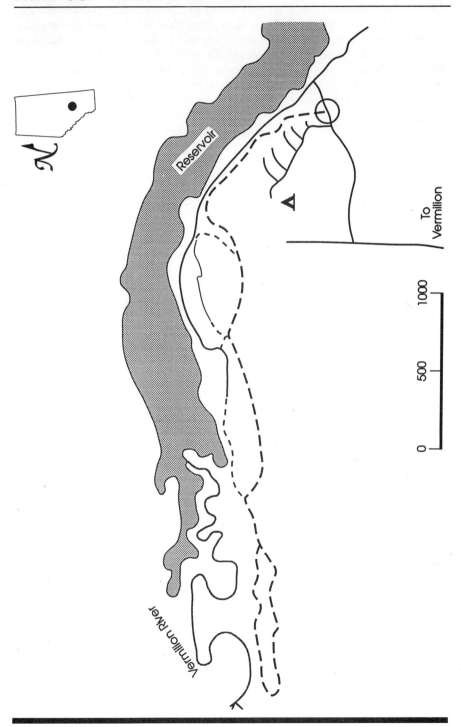

Reservoir

Vermilion River

To Vermilion

0   500   1000

As the trail leaves the woods and enters a more arid meadow, look for clumps of wild rose, buckbrush, and chokecherry. Turn left onto the Wolfwillow Trail, which is named for a silver-leaved plant common to the grassy meadows. Most of the grass is rough fescue sprinkled with prairie sage, three-flowered avens, and northern bedstraw. Follow the Wolfwillow Trail across the grassy plateau for 600 metres to the junction with the Wild Rose and Fescue trails and bear straight ahead onto the Lakeside road. Walk along the road for 300 metres to the end of the pavement and continue on the Lakeside Trail. You can replenish your water bottles at the picnic area just north of the gate at the end of the road.

The Lakeside Trail skirts close to the upper end of the reservoir, with good opportunities for viewing teal, bufflehead, widgeon, and other waterfowl. Watch for great blue heron fishing in the shallows. Within 500 metres, the trail forks east and west. Continue west to complete the Cathedral Loop, a two-kilometre trek through aspen forest. Balsam poplar thrive on the moist north-facing slopes here, along with red osier dogwood and a few spruce trees. The moist conditions also encourage raspberries and broadleaf strawberries.

On the return trip, you can avoid retracing your steps by following the Wild Rose Trail, which then crosses the Wolfwillow Trail to join the Fescue Trail heading east. The Fescue Trail covers more than a kilometre of open meadow, with good views of the reservoir and a chance to see red-tailed and swainson's hawks as they hunt for ground squirrels and other small mammals in the grass. At the end of the Fescue Trail, turn left onto the Wolfwillow Trail and follow the Aspen Trail back to the trailhead.

Elk Island National Park

Originally established as an elk preserve in 1906, Elk Island was not designated as a national park until 1930. In the intervening years it became a sanctuary not only for elk, but for plains and wood bison, moose, lynx, beaver, coyote, and over 230 species of birds. Today the park encompasses 195 square kilometres and contains Canada's largest herd of plains bison as well as a smaller herd of the rare wood bison.

Many visitors to Elk Island's trails come in the winter for the excellent cross-country skiing, but summer hiking is growing in popularity. Trails are generally flat or rolling over the hillocky terrain left by the last ice age 12,000 years ago. Sections of trail can be boggy or inundated due to seasonal flooding or beaver activity. With numerous lakes and wetlands, Elk Island is a haven for waterfowl, shorebirds, and flies and mosquitoes. The best time of year for hiking is late August and September, though spring has its own rewards if trails are passable. For current information, contact the Park Superintendent, Elk Island National Park, R.R. #1, Site 4, Fort Saskatchewan, Alberta, T8L 2N7.

HIKE 31 *WOOD BISON TRAIL*

General description: A moderate day hike through the poplar forest and open meadows around Flyingshot Lake.

General location: In the southern section of Elk Island National Park, forty-five kilometres east of Edmonton.

Maps: Elk Island National Park; Elk Island 83 H/10.

Special attractions: Flyingshot Lake, waterfowl, good chance of seeing wood bison.

For more information: Park Superintendent, Elk Island National Park, R.R. #1, Site 4, Fort Saskatchewan, Alberta, T8L 2N7. Ph: (403) 992-5790. For a tape recorded message about the park's trails, phone (403) 922-5790.

Finding the trailhead: From Edmonton, drive forty-five kilometres east on the Yellowhead Highway (16) to the intersection with the park entrance road. Turn right (south) and proceed through the high fence, then to the right again and park in the lot at the wood bison interpretive exhibit next to the trailhead.

The hike: Elk Island National Park covers 195 square kilometres of the Beaver Hills, a forested, boggy remnant of the last ice age. As the continental glacier retreated, ice remained and melted in the pockets and hollows formed in the mounds of rocky debris. Today the park is laced with shallow lakes and innumerable beaver ponds set in a patchwork of poplar forests and grassy meadows.

At nineteen kilometres, the Wood Bison Trail is the longest hiking loop in Elk Island National Park. It is also the only designated hiking trail in the

Wood Bison in Elk Island National Park.

southern section of the park, and offers the best chance of seeing the rare wood bison in its natural habitat. The park also hosts Canada's largest herd of the plains bison, which roam the land on the north side of the Yellowhead Highway.

Be prepared for wet sections of trail due to seasonal flooding or beaver activity. Also carry a lunch and plenty of drinking water, and douse yourself well in insect repellent. Bird watchers will want binoculars and a field guide

HIKE 31 *WOOD BISON*

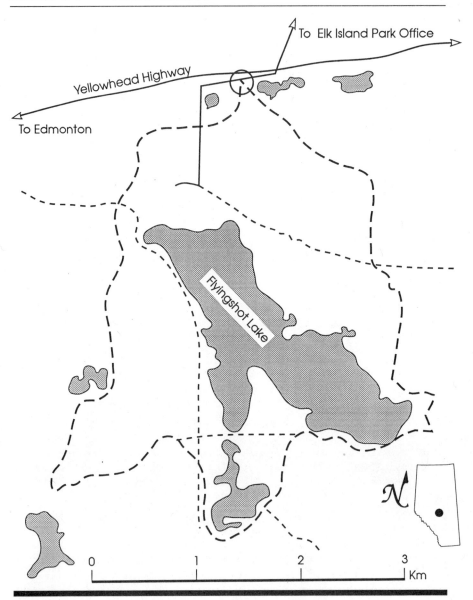

to better study any of the park's 230 bird species. Also watch for coyote, moose, elk, white-tailed deer, and beaver.

The loop can be hiked in either direction, though heading to the right from the parking lot leads more quickly to Flyingshot Lake. Just over two kilometres from the trailhead, the trail intersects a road; turn left and walk about 600 metres (following the righthand track where the road forks) to the lakeshore for bird watching. Backtrack to the main trail to continue the Wood Bison loop.

In another two kilometres, the trail enters a hilly section, skirting a small lake to the west and then reaching another road junction. Turn left and follow the rolling trail east then south to a narrows between the southernmost arm of Flyingshot Lake and a low marshy area. From here, the route beelines back to the shore of Flyingshot Lake, rounds its southeast end, and breaks north from a cutline that continues east. The remaining four kilometres are an easy stroll through sun-dappled poplar stands.

Wood bison may be seen anywhere on this loop, though they often congregate in clearings near the western and northeastern legs of the trail. Remember that all bison are wild animals and potentially dangerous. The wood bison is the largest native land mammal in North America and can move with surprising quickness and agility. Do not hike through a herd and do not approach individuals. Bulls are particularly aggressive during the rut, from late July through late August, and cows will charge if their calves appear to be threatened. Also leave your pets at home—dogs are not allowed on any trails within Elk Island National Park. Enjoy the mighty bison from a safe distance and bring a telephoto lens if you want a close-up portrait.

HIKE 32   *HAYBURGER TRAIL*

General description: An easy day hike through a spruce bog, aspen parkland, and open meadows.
General location: Near the middle of Elk Island National Park, forty-five kilometres east of Edmonton.
Maps: Elk Island National Park; Elk Island 83 H/10.
Special attractions: One of the drier hikes in the park, wildlife viewing.
For more information: Park Superintendent, Elk Island National Park, R.R. #1, Site 4, Fort Saskatchewan, Alberta, T8L 2N7. Ph: (403) 992-5790. For a tape recorded message about the park's trails, phone (403) 922-5790.
Finding the trailhead: From Edmonton, drive forty-five kilometres east on the Yellowhead Highway (16) to the Elk Island National Park entrance. Turn left (north) and follow the main park road seven kilometres to the Hayburger Trail parking lot on the east side of the road. The trail begins just beyond the interpretive exhibit by the parking lot.

The hike: The Hayburger Trail traverses relatively flat terrain and a variety of plant communities in its twelve kilometres. This loop skirts only one small lake, near the halfway point, and (in a good year) much of the track is well-drained and dry—a change of pace from many of the park's trails.

The first kilometre, however, can be damp as it bisects a spruce bog before reaching the loop intersection. Turn left and follow the undulating trail through aspen stands and several more bogs, gradually angling south onto flatter ground. Near the midpoint, the trail slices through large open meadows, a good place to see deer, coyotes, and plains bison. Watch for elk in the early morning near meadow's edge.

As the trail curves westward it passes a small lake to the north. Several

HIKE 32 *HAYBURGER*

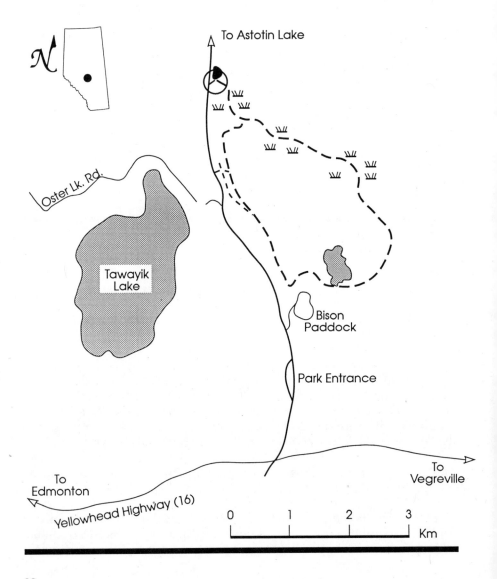

spur trails lead closer to the lake, a good spot for observing waterfowl and muskrat. From here the trail continues west along the fenceline then north, parallel to the park road. Stay to the right at the fork with the old road bed and continue straight for the next two kilometres to reach the end of the loop and the short walk back to the parking lot.

This hike is best in the early morning when deer, elk, and bison are more active and likely to be in the open.

Cooking Lake Hills

Canada's first forest preserve, established in 1899, included the area now protected as the Cooking Lake-Blackfoot Recreation, Wildlife, and Grazing Area. This ninety-seven square kilometre area lies thirty kilometres east of Edmonton, directly south of Elk Island National Park. This guide describes four trail systems within the area's boundaries, a disproportionate number for such a small area, because the Cooking Lake Hills are largely unknown to hikers. Over ninety kilometres of hiking trails traverse the irregular landscape of hills and kettles, innumerable lakes and beaver ponds, and dense forests of aspen and balsam poplar.

Wildlife residents include mule and white-tailed deer, elk, and moose; coyote, red fox, cougar, and lynx, and over 220 species of birds. Waterfowl are abundant as are shorebirds and song birds, and an observant hiker will likely see woodpeckers, red-tailed hawks, osprey, and great blue heron.

The area is open for day use only from 7:00 a.m. to 11:00 p.m. daily. The hiking season runs from late May (when some trails are flooded by snow-melt and runoff) to September. Hunting is allowed within the area's boundaries in the fall, but the season varies year to year. Contact the park staff at the Cooking Lake-Blackfoot Grazing, Wildlife, and Recreation Area, P.O. Box 57104, Sherwood Park, Alberta, T8A 5L7. Ph: (403) 922-3293.

HIKE 33 BLACKFOOT LAKE

General description: An easy day hike through the poplar forests and beaver ponds of the Cooking Lake Hills.
General location: East of Elk Island National Park, fifty kilometres east of downtown Edmonton.
Maps: Elk Island National Park; Alberta Parks and Recreation Trail Guide.
Special attractions: Deer, elk, moose, beaver, waterfowl, great blue heron rookery, numerous lakes and ponds.
For more information: Park Ranger, Cooking Lake-Blackfoot Grazing, Wildlife, and Provincial Recreation Area, P.O. Box 57104, Sherwood Park, Alberta, T8A 5L7. Ph: (403) 922-3293.

HIKE 33 *BLACKFOOT LAKE*

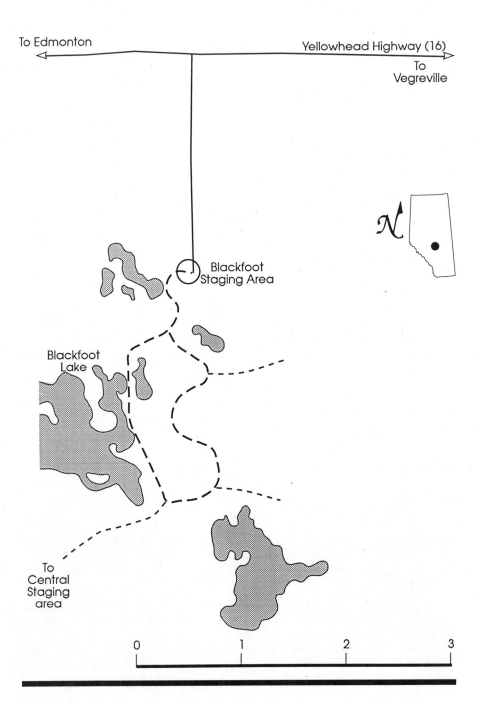

Finding the trailhead: The Blackfoot Lake Staging Area lies just east of the southern third of Elk Island National Park. From Edmonton, drive east for fifty kilometres on the Yellowhead Highway (16). About 800 metres beyond the access road into the Ukrainian Cultural Heritage Village, turn right and continue for 3.5 kilometres to the staging area and parking lot. The hiking trail begins to the right of the parking lot, past a locked gate at the edge of the woods.

The hike: The Blackfoot Lake region of the Cooking Lake-Blackfoot Provincial Recreation Area contains over seventeen kilometres of hiking trails. Most of these trails tend to remain drier than trails in other sections of the recreation area and so provide better early season hiking opportunities.

The main attraction on the Blackfoot Lake Trail is a large heron rookery on an island near the eastern shore of Blackfoot Lake. The rookery is reached in an easy 2.5 kilometre walk, but most hikers enjoy trekking around the complete six-kilometre loop.

Follow the trail south for slightly over 500 metres, then turn right at the first trail junction. After another 400 metres the trail drops down between an unnamed slough on the left and an arm of Blackfoot Lake on the right. This section may be wet. Proceed down the trail to the slight rise at the far end of the slough. The heron rookery can be seen in the trees lining the shore of the island in Blackfoot Lake. Great blue heron begin arriving in May and nest at the site through early summer. Binoculars will give you a closer look at the long-legged birds in their stick nests.

To complete the loop, continue south for another 1.5 kilometres to a junction with an equestrian trail heading west. Turn left here and walk for 500 metres to another trail junction. Bear left again. Walk north through the mixed forest for two kilometres to rejoin the main trail to the staging area.

A corner of Blackfoot Lake near a heron rookery in the Cooking Lake Hills.

HIKE 34 *BLACKFOOT BACKCOUNTRY*

General description: An moderate day hike through the poplar forests and around beaver ponds in the Cooking Lake Hills.
General location: East of Elk Island National Park, forty kilometres east of downtown Edmonton.

HIKE 34 *BLACKFOOT BACKCOUNTRY*

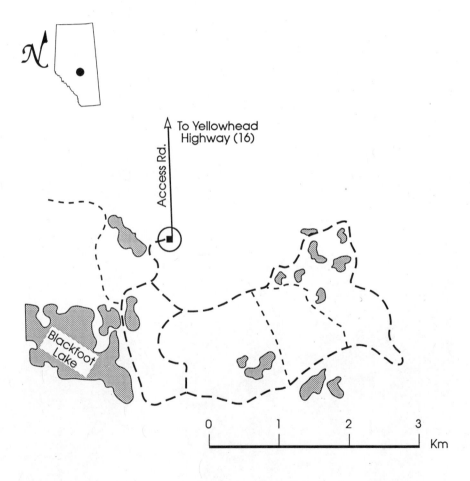

Maps: Elk Island National Park; Alberta Parks and Recreation Trail Guide.
Special attractions: Deer, elk, moose, beaver, waterfowl, numerous lakes and ponds.
For more information: Park Ranger, Cooking Lake-Blackfoot Grazing, Wildlife, and Provincial Recreation Area, P.O. Box 57104, Sherwood Park, Alberta, T8A 5L7. Ph: (403) 922-3293.
Finding the Trailhead: The Blackfoot Lake Staging Area lies just east of the southern third of Elk Island National Park. From Edmonton, drive east for forty kilometres on the Yellowhead Highway (16). About 800 metres beyond the access road into the Ukranian Cultural Heritage Village, turn right and continue for three and a half kilometres to the staging area and parking lot. The hiking trail begins directly south of the parking lot, east of the locked gate and access road.

The hike: Hikers looking for solitude have a good chance to find it on the backcountry trails east of Blackfoot Lake in the Cooking Lake-Blackfoot Provincial Recreation Area. Most visitors to this staging area come to see Blackfoot Lake and its heron rookery (see Hike 33 Blackfoot Lake), but an additional ten kilometres of rugged trails beckon to the avid hiker.

The foot and equestrian trail heads south for 300 metres before angling east for nearly one kilometre to a junction with the Muskrat trail. Turn left and left again in 100 metres to stay on the Blackfoot trail. From here the trail rolls through dense poplar and aspen forests with thick undergrowth. Look for strawberries, raspberries, and saskatoon berries for a handy snack.

This leg of the loop also skirts the edges of several marshes and beaver ponds; sections of the trail may be wet or boggy. Eventually the trail angles south, with a few short uphill grades to drier ground. After four kilometres, turn right at the next junction and walk west for one kilometre to the junction with the Elkhorn trail. Look for the hiker's shelter a few metres up the Elkhorn trail, which also offers the shortest route back to the trailhead, a distance of about three kilometres.

Hardy hikers can continue west on the Blackfoot trail another three kilometres to the Whitetail trail, a wide, grassy access road, which bears north along the shores of Blackfoot Lake for 2.8 kilometres to the staging area. Watch for waterfowl and wading birds in the lake and deer and songbirds at the forest's edge.

HIKE 35 *ISLET LAKE TO WANISAN LAKE*

General description: A moderate day hike through the wetlands and poplar forests of the Cooking Lake Hills.
General location: South of Elk Island National Park, thirty-five kilometres east of Edmonton.
Maps: Elk Island National Park; Provincial Recreation Area Trail Guide.
Special attractions: Numerous lakes and ponds, beaver activity, deer, elk, moose, abundant waterfowl.

HIKE 35 *ISLET LAKE*

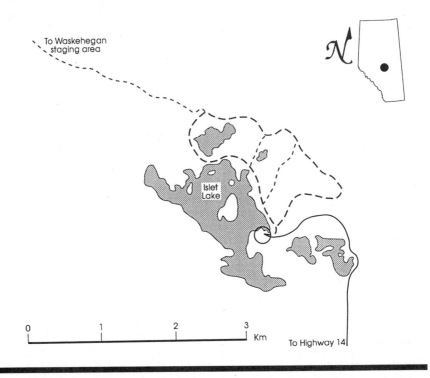

For more information: Park Ranger, Cooking Lake-Blackfoot Grazing, Wildlife, and Provincial Recreation Area, P.O. Box 57104, Sherwood Park, Alberta, T8A 5L7. Ph: (403) 922-3293.

Finding the trailhead: The Islet Lake Staging Area is reached by twisting through a maze of unlikely backroads. From Edmonton, follow the Yellowhead Highway (16) east for thirty kilometres toward Elk Island National Park. Turn right on Range Road 210 and drive 11.5 kilometres to the small village of North Cooking Lake. Turn left on Highway 630 and then left again in two kilometres on Wye Road. Beware: most of the secondary roads in this area are apparently named Wye Road. Stay on the main road, bearing east for four kilometres, then angling southeast, then east again for another three kilometres. As the road turns south again, look for the provincial recreation area sign and take the access road to the left, following it north for two kilometres to the staging area on the shores of Islet Lake.

The hike: The Cooking Lake Hills formed some 12,500 years ago as the last of the continental glaciers receded, leaving behind large mounds of silt, sand, and gravel interspersed with water-filled depressions. This "kettle-and-moraine" landscape now supports a lush poplar forest sprinkled with lakes and wetlands, superb habitat for beaver, waterfowl, deer, elk, and moose.

The trails radiating from the Islet Lake Staging Area lead hikers into the heart of the hills, and the trails are perhaps the most challenging within the Cooking Lake-Blackfoot Recreation Area. The nineteen-kilometre loop to Wanisan Lake skirts marshy lakeshores, then climbs aspen-covered knobs only to give way to boggy lowlands again. Mosquitoes and flies can be voracious by mid-summer, and hikers should be on the lookout for yellow-jacket nests. Despite these difficulties, a day on the trails in the Cooking Lake Hills will reward even the casual hiker with wildlife, scenic views, bird songs, and long stretches of solitude.

The trail begins at the north end of the parking lot and parallels the road for 400 metres. At the first trail junction, bear left, following the east shore of the lake. Turn left at the next two junctions and cross the narrows between Islet Lake and an unnamed pond to the north. Watch for waterfowl and shorebirds taking wing as you skirt the lake.

At the next trail junction, turn left and head northwest through the opening in the ungulate fence. These fences prevent moose and elk from leaving the area, helping to stabilize their populations. Take a right at the next trail junction and follow this northern trail for five kilometres to the junction with the Lost Lake Trail (see Hike 36). The poplar forest here provides food and cover for deer, coyote, fox, lynx, and cougar. Winged residents include great horned and great gray owls, goshawks, and cooper's hawks.

To return to Islet Lake, head south through the ungulate fence again and along the shores of Wanisan Lake. There are several good spots by the lake for rest and lunch. After skirting a marshy area midway down the lake, the trail turns north and east again, recrossing the fenceline and rolling through hills and around several beaver ponds. Stay to the right at the next two trail junctions to rejoin the Push Lake Trail roughly three kilometres north of the staging area.

HIKE 36 *LOST LAKE LOOP*

General description: An easy day hike through the poplar forest and beaver ponds of the Cooking Lake Hills.
General location: South of Elk Island National Park, thirty kilometres east of Edmonton.
Maps: Elk Island National Park; Alberta Parks and Recreation Trail Guide.
Special attractions: Deer, elk, moose, beaver, waterfowl, numerous lakes and ponds.
For more information: Park Ranger, Cooking Lake-Blackfoot Grazing, Wildlife, and Provincial Recreation Area, P.O. Box 57104, Sherwood Park, Alberta, T8A 5L7. Ph: (403) 922-3293.
Finding the trailhead: To reach the trailhead from Edmonton, drive east on the Yellowhead Highway (16) about thirty kilometres. After crossing Route 830, watch for Alberta Parks and Recreation signs and Range Road 210. Turn right on Range Road 210 and head south for seven kilometres. Turn left onto

the Staging Area access road and drive to the parking lot at the end. Horse riders and their rigs tend to congregate around the equestrian trailhead at the north end of the parking lot, so look for space at the other end, near the picnic tables. The Lost Lake trail begins at the edge of the woods behind the picnic area.

The hike: The Lost Lake Loop begins at the Waskehegan Staging Area on the

HIKE 36 *LOST LAKE TRAIL/WANISAN LAKE*

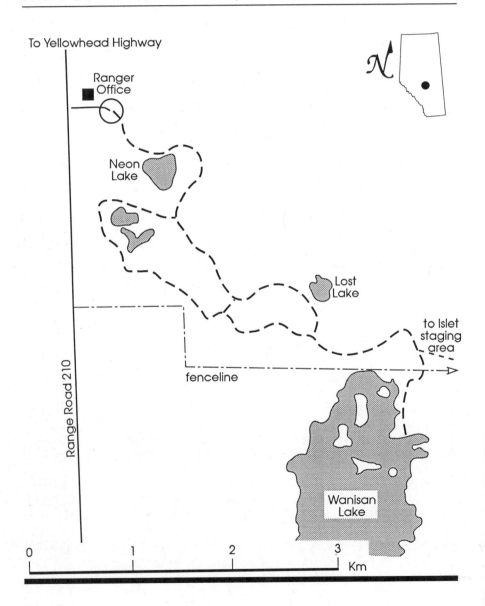

western edge of the Cooking Lake-Blackfoot provincial recreation area. Only thirty-two kilometres from Edmonton, Waskehegan is one of the more popular hiking and equestrian trailheads in the Cooking Lake Hills, but early risers will often find empty trails.

The Lost Lake Loop travels over gently rolling hills through dense poplar forest and past innumerable beaver ponds, affording good opportunities to watch beaver at work. The lakes, sloughs, and ponds also teem with waterfowl and the surrounding woods are home to a variety of songbirds. You may also see deer, elk, and moose. Trails are wide and grassy with some wet or muddy sections in low-lying areas. Bring a good supply of drinking water from home (water at the trailhead is potable but unpleasant) and douse yourself in insect repellent, particularly during July and early August.

For an enjoyable twelve-kilometre loop hike, bear left at the first trail junction 300 metres from the trailhead. Each junction is posted with a detailed trail map of the area, and all of the trails are posted by name. Following the sequence of Lost Lake signs takes you north along the shores of Neon Lake and then south through dense stands of poplar. Continue bearing left at the next two trail junctions until you reach Lost Lake. A bench with a roof overhead makes a good resting point overlooking the lake.

From Lost Lake, head south for 200 metres and turn left again. Within a kilometre the trail joins the Waskehegan Trail heading north, and then the Meadow Trail angling east to the Islet Lake Staging Area (see Hike 35–Islet Lake). Continue south past both of these junctions to an opening in the ungulate fence. From here the trail climbs a low ridge with views east and south to Wanisan Lake. It is less than 500 metres from the first glimpse of Wanisan Lake on the ridge to the lake's northeastern shore. Stop at Wanisan Lake for lunch and some leisurely bird watching.

The return route backtracks through the ungulate fence and west to the trail junction directly south of Lost Lake. Take the Grouse Trail to the left and bear left at the next three junctions to return to the trailhead. This return route is about one kilometre longer than the first leg.

Miquelon Lake Provincial Park

HIKE 37   *MIQUELON 2*

General description: An easy day hike on well-maintained trails to a lake teeming with shore birds and other waterfowl.
General location: Forty minutes southeast of Edmonton in Miquelon Lake Provincial Park.
Maps: Miquelon Lake Provincial Park map and brochure.
Special attractions: Bird watching, moose, deer, beaver; fishing, swimming, developed recreation facilities nearby.

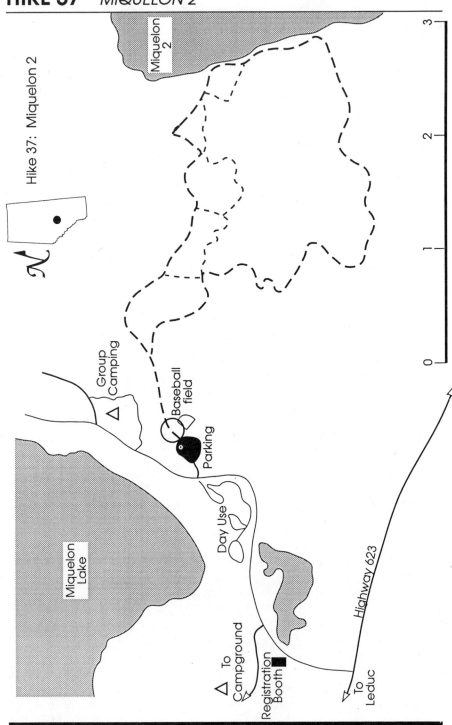

Hike 37: Miquelon 2

For more information: Miquelon Lake Provincial Park, Box 1977, Camrose, Alberta, T4V 1X8. Ph: (403) 672-7308.

Finding the trailhead: To get to Miquelon Lake Provincial Park from Edmonton, head out of town on Highway 14. Turn south on Highway 21 and drive about twenty-five kilometres to the junction with Highway 623. Turn east and continue for twenty kilometres to the park entrance road on the left. Day visitors can drive past the park entrance booth and campground access road to the large parking lot on the right, just beyond the road to the park administrator's office. Walk up the hill to the northeast corner of the parking lot, following a grass-covered road between the baseball diamond and the group camping area. The trailhead is marked with a sign and map next to an outhouse.

The hike: Miquelon Lake Provincial Park offers a wide range of recreational opportunities, attracting crowds of visitors from nearby Camrose and Edmonton during the summer. Developed facilities at Miquelon include a swimming beach, sport fields, boat ramps, picnic areas, and campgrounds. A network of hiking trails connects the main lake with its smaller namesake to the east, Miquelon 2.

The trail is wide and grassy, regularly mowed by park staff after the spring waters have receded. Each major trail junction is posted with a detailed map of the trail network and a snowflake symbol indicating your present location. The most enjoyable route to Miquelon 2 follows the outermost trails, always bearing to the left at each trail junction. This eight-kilometre loop takes you past numerous beaver ponds and over low hills to the flat, marshy western shore of Miquelon 2, some 3.5 kilometres from the trailhead.

You'll want to move quietly as you near the lake to better your chances of spotting moose, deer, and wading birds in the shallows. The shore can be wet and ankle deep in muck, especially early in the season. Also be prepared for mosquitoes, ticks, and flies. But the bird watching more than makes up for such hardships. The park bird checklist includes white pelicans, great blue herons, black-crowned night herons, tundra swans, teal, goldeneyes, mergansers, grebes, sandhill cranes, plover, yellowlegs, an array of sandpipers, eagles, osprey, and great horned owls. Summer visitors are likely to see kettles of gulls near the park entrance; chickadees, ruffed grouse, and northern orioles in the woods; northern harriers and red-tailed hawks hunting the marshes; and killdeer and avocet on the shores of Miquelon 2.

On the return trip from Miquelon 2, follow the shoreline for 500 metres then turn into the forest again. A four-kilometre trail winds south and west, much of it on higher ground than the first leg of the loop. An abandoned barn marks the halfway point between Miquelon 2 and the trailhead. Watch for moose and elk in the meadows along the trail, particularly in the early morning or evening.

Dinosaur Provincial Park

HIKE 38   *BADLANDS TRAIL*

General description: An easy day hike along a short interpretive trail through the badlands of the Red Deer Valley.

General location: In the centre of Dinosaur Provincial Park, southeastern Alberta.

Maps: Badlands Trail brochure.

Special attractions: The rugged, eroded features of a true badlands, numerous birds, cactus and other desert plants.

For more information: Dinosaur Provincial Park, Box 60, Patricia, Alberta, TOJ 2KO. Ph: (403) 378-4587.

Finding the trailhead: Dinosaur Provincial Park lies north of the Trans Canada Highway near Brooks, Alberta. To reach the park, turn north on Highway 36 where it crosses the Trans Canada Highway about eight kilometres west of Brooks. After five kilometres, turn east onto Highway 544 and continue for twenty-three kilometres to the park access road on the left. Follow this road for sixteen kilometres north and east to the main entrance. Campers staying at the park can easily walk to the trailhead by following the

Hikers on the Badlands Trail in Dinosaur Provincial Park.

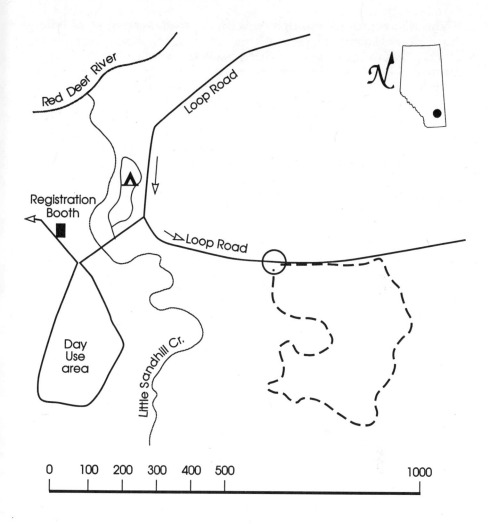

beginning of the one-way loop road just south of the campground. Day-use visitors can park at the trailhead. Drive past the rangers' booth and bear left across the bridge over Little Sandhill Creek. Continue straight past the campground entrance and then turn right onto the loop road. The Badlands Trail parking lot is on the left, about 200 metres from the bridge.

The hike: Although the Badlands Interpretive Trail is only 1.5 kilometres long, it dips, rolls, and snakes its way through a colourful landscape the entire family will enjoy. The hike is also highly educational: fifteen numbered stations along the way correspond to descriptions of natural features in the trail brochure available at the trailhead. Take your camera, sunglasses, and a hat to keep your head cool—temperatures of 47° C., in the shade, have been recorded in the park.

The trail begins on the right side of the road, bearing south into a moonscape of balanced rocks and sandstone mounds etched with rills and crevices. Scant vegetation grows here, but keep an eye out for prickly pear cactus and bull thistle. The cactus produces a showy yellow or magenta bloom during late spring and early summer, but watch your step. The cactus's thorns can puncture the sole of a misplaced tennis shoe.

As the trail wends through gullies and over scoured layers of sandstone and clay, follow your progress in the interpretive brochure. It describes all of the erosional features and the processes that shaped them, allowing attentive hikers to better appreciate their surroundings. Armed with this new knowledge, many hikers continue their walk beyond the end of the trail. The Badlands Trail rejoins the loop road about 100 metres east of the trailhead.

Park staff conduct guided hikes of the badlands south and east of the trail, but it is otherwise closed to the public. The area within the loop road is open to the public, but take care to avoid trampling plants or fragile features. Take only photographs, and leave all fossils and rocks untouched so future hikers can also enjoy the treasures of the park, which was declared a UNESCO World Heritage Site in 1979.

HIKE 39   COTTONWOOD FLATS

General description: An easy day hike on a well-maintained interpretive trail.
General location: Along the Red Deer River in Dinosaur Provincial Park, southeastern Alberta.
Maps: Cottonwood Trail park brochure.
Special attractions: The Red Deer River, riparian plants, great blue herons, songbirds.
For more information: Dinosaur Provincial Park, Box 60, Patricia, Alberta, TOJ 2KO. Ph: (403) 378-4587.
Finding the trailhead: The Cottonwood Flats Trail begins just north of the campground. Drive past the park rangers' booth and turn right into the parking lot for the day-use area. Walk north across the bridge of Little Sandhill Creek, past the campground entrance, and bear left along the one-way loop road. The trailhead is about 200 metres from the bridge. If you wish to park at the trailhead, you can drive the three-kilometre loop road, turning right into the small parking lot just before completing the loop.

The hike: Dinosaur Provincial Park attracts thousands of visitors each year who come to see its badlands and fossil beds, but the park is also popular with bird watchers. The Cottonwood Flats trail provides excellent access to

HIKE 39 *COTTONWOOD FLATS*

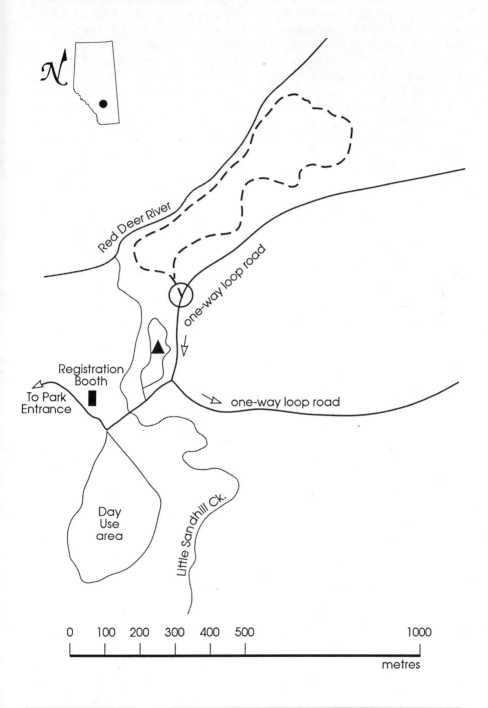

one of the best birding spots in the park, the brushy, tree-covered floodplain along the Red Deer River.

The trail immediately drops onto the mudflats on the south bank of the Red Deer River. Rain can turn the trail into a greasy gumbo, so the trail is best avoided after a thundershower. Be sure to pick up a trail brochure at the trailhead, and follow your progress from station to station by reading the corresponding descriptions in the brochure. The interpretive hike focuses on the plants and animals living in this narrow riparian corridor between the river and the arid badlands above. The lush vegetation here offers food and shelter for mule and white-tailed deer, porcupine, beaver, and rabbits.

Bird watchers will thrill to the crackle of the belted kingfisher and the raspy call of the great blue heron. Northern orioles frequent the upper canopy of the cottonwoods, while chickadees, woodpeckers, and northern flickers dart from tree to tree. The great horned owl is a common summer resident of the cottonwood stands.

To see more of the river, stay to the left as you begin the 1.5 kilometre loop. On the return leg, the trail twines its way through a brushy, arid zone of greasewood, sagebrush, and grasses. Amid the scatter of sneaker treads and Vibram sole prints, look for the record of animals' passing in the dried mud along the entire route—the web of goose or a beaver's hind foot, the teardrop of a deer's hooves, or the oval pads of a cottontail. Most of these animals are under cover during the heat of day, but the impressionable ground reveals their ways and habits to the careful observer.

Cypress Hills Provincial Park

HIKE 40   SPRUCE COULEE

General description: A moderate day hike or overnight on the Cypress Hills plateau.

General location: Near the northern boundary of Cypress Hills Provincial Park in southeastern Alberta.

Maps: Cypress Hills Provincial Park trail brochure; 72E/9.

Special attractions: Beaver ponds, wildlife, Spruce Coulee Reservoir.

For more information: Park Superintendent, Cypress Hills Provincial Park, Elkwater, Alberta TOJ 1CO. Ph: (403) 893-3833.

Finding the trailhead: The trailhead lies just east of the town of Elkwater. From town, head south on Highway 41. You will immediately pass the access road to the rodeo grounds on the left. Within 200 metres a dirt road on the left leads to a small parking area and the trailhead sign. If you don't intend to hike back along the same trail, have someone drive to the Spruce Coulee Campground at the other end of the trail, or arrange a shuttle.

The hike: After crossing the miles of treeless, rolling plains surrounding the Cypress Hills, visitors are usually eager to immerse themselves in the dense, verdant forest carpeting the north-facing slopes. The eight-kilometre Spruce Coulee Trail is perhaps the best point from which to dive in. The trail wanders through spruce and poplar forest, with occasional openings offering views of the distant plains.

Initially the trail follows an abandoned road on open slopes above a small ravine. At 2.5 kilometres the main trail intersects with the Rodeo Trail on the left, which leads back to the rodeo grounds, and the Highline Trail on the right, which loops back to join the main trail near the trailhead. Both of these side trails are groomed for cross-country skiing through the winter.

The main trail continues east, narrowing to a single track as it enters a dense, shadowy forest of spruce. Near the halfway point the trail ascends a small, bald knob crowned with aspen, offering excellent views of the northern face of the Cypress Hills and of the plains beyond. After roughly seven kilometres the trail crosses Bull Trail Road, the access road to Spruce Coulee Reservoir. Stay to the right as you drop down the east side of the road bank—there are numerous side trails and game runs threading through the brush. Watch for helpful trail signs.

Another kilometre of hiking brings you to a junction with the Lakeside Trail just fifty metres above the Spruce Coulee Campground. A picnic shelter, fire pits, toilets, and drinking water are available at the campground. Although the trail can easily be hiked in a couple of hours, camping at Spruce Coulee would make it a comfortable overnight with plenty of spare time for fishing at the reservoir.

HIKE 40 *SPRUCE COULEE TRAIL*

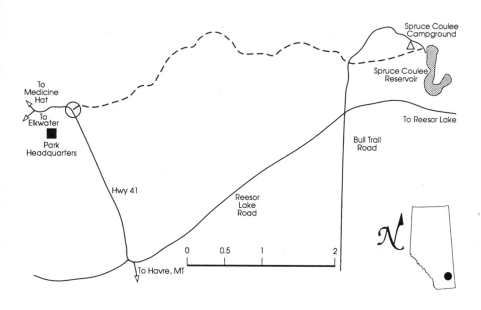

HIKE 41 *STREAMSIDE*

General description: An easy, rambling loop through spruce forests to the top of the Cypress Hills Plateau.

General location: East of the Spruce Coulee Reservoir in Cypress Hills Provincial Park.

Maps: Cypress Hills Provincial Park trail brochure; 72 E/9.

Special attractions: Beaver ponds, wildlife, views atop the plateau.

For more information: Park Superintendent, Cypress Hills Provincial Park, Elkwater, Alberta T0J 1C0. Ph: (403) 893-3833.

Finding the trailhead: From Elkwater Lake, take Highway 41 south about 2.5 kilometres to the junction with the Reesor Lake Road. Turn left and follow the Reesor Lake Road four kilometres to the junction with the Bull Trail Road. Turn left again and drive about five kilometres to the Spruce Coulee parking lot at the end of the road. The trail, marked with a sign, starts just below the parking lot.

The hike: This five-kilometre loop crosses a variety of terrain and woodland habitats, providing a good sampling of the Cypress Hills landscape. Allow

HIKE 41 *STREAMSIDE*

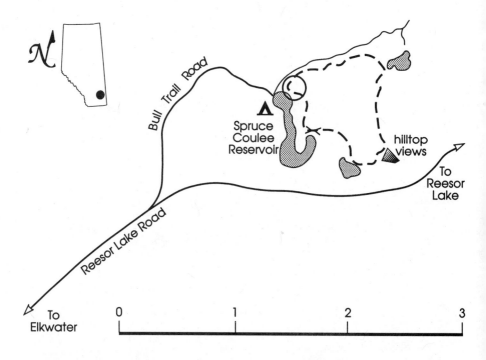

two to three hours for the hike—to better enjoy the flora and fauna, and to allow for a slower pace on the climb onto the plateau.

Parts of this trail are narrow and bushy, muddy in the spring or after a rain, and sometimes challenging to follow. For all that, the hike is not difficult and the observant hiker will be rewarded with a glimpse of a less tame corner of the Cypress Hills.

The trail drops immediately into the ravine cut by the outflow from Spruce Coulee Reservoir. As the stream wends east, the trail jogs along the densely forested southern bank, frequently climbing the hillside and then dipping down to the stream again. The spruce forest eventually gives way to stands of aspen and the trail skirts a small string of beaver ponds. After angling south, the trail breaks into a marshy meadow surrounding a larger pond. Look for geese, ducks, and great blue heron in the shallows. Elk and deer also come to this basin for the lush forage and good protective cover.

Leading south, the trail crosses a small stream—you have a choice of downed logs to reach the other bank—and then climbs steadily through a mixed spruce and aspen forest to the top of the Cypress Hills plateau. Go quietly near the top where the forest and upper meadows meet and you may spot grazing white-tailed deer before they bound away.

Once in the meadow, the trail meanders like a game run, curving east near the top of a low grassy knoll. There are good views of the plateau before the trail drops down to the outlet stream of a large beaver impounded lake. The trail swings along the north shore, a grassy slope good for a lunch stop. Muskrats and waterfowl are common here.

From this lake, the trail climbs back onto the open plateau only to descend again to one arm of Spruce Coulee Reservoir. A wooden bridge leads across

A beaver pond atop Cypress Hills plateau, along the Streamside Trail.

the arm, but the ground is often soggy, particularly in spring. Bear right for a drier crossing on an earthen berm. From here, the ruts of an old road head north on the hillside above the reservoir, finally crossing the causeway back to the parking lot. Remember to check your legs and clothing for ticks and burrs before getting in your car.

HIKE 42 *LAKESIDE*

General description: An easy stroll through a mixed conifer forest on the shores of Spruce Coulee Reservoir.
General location: Near the northeast end of Cypress Hills Provincial Park in southeastern Alberta.
Maps: Cypress Hills Provincial Park trail brochure; 72 E/9.
Special attractions: Fishing, woodland plants, and wildlife.
For more information: Park Superintendent, Cypress Hills Provincial Park, Elkwater, Alberta TOJ 1CO. Ph: (403) 893-3833.
Finding the trailhead: To get to Spruce Coulee Reservoir from Elkwater Lake, take Highway 41 south about 2.5 kilometres to the junction with the

HIKE 42 *LAKESIDE*

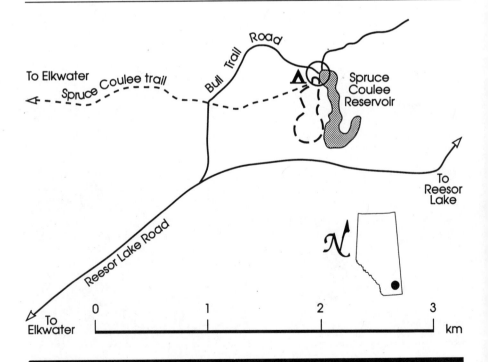

Reesor Lake Road. Turn left and follow the Reesor Lake Road four kilometres to the junction with the Bull Trail Road. Turn left again and drive about five kilometres to the Spruce Coulee parking lot at the end of the road.

The hike: The Lakeside trail is a good choice for an evening stroll for families staying at the Spruce Coulee Campground. The two-kilometre loop begins near the picnic shelter in the campground and wanders through the forest, never straying far from the reservoir. Anglers looking to avoid the tangle of fishing lines along the causeway use the lower leg of the loop to reach the far end of the reservoir.

The short access road into the campground is closed to vehicles, so walk around the gate and up to the picnic shelter. Continue past a water pump and a campsite to the trail sign. The trail leads south into a thick forest of spruce and lodgepole pine and immediately joins the Spruce Coulee Trail. Bear left at this junction.

At the halfway point, the trail turns eastward and meanders down to the reservoir's southernmost end. This leg of the loop receives heavier use because of the fishing access it provides, but bird watchers will also enjoy the terrain. Watch for dark-eyed juncoes and nuthatches in the woods, and teal, mallards, and grebes on the water. Follow the trail northward above the reservoir to return to the campground.

HIKE 43   *HORSESHOE CANYON VIEWPOINT*

General description: A moderately strenuous day hike or overnight through open fields and mixed woodlands.
General location: South of Elkwater Lake in Cypress Hills Provincial Park.
Maps: Cypress Hills Provincial Park trail brochure; 72E/9.
Special attractions: Horseshoe Canyon Viewpoint 500 metres above surrounding plains; diversity of wildlife habitats.
For more information: Park Superintendent, Cypress Hills Provincial Park, Elkwater, Alberta T0J 1C0. Ph: (403) 893-3833.
Finding the trailhead:

The hike: Horseshoe Canyon trail follows an abandoned roadway that climbs 200 metres in elevation from Elkwater Lake along the flank of Old Baldy to the top of the Cypress Hills plateau. The hike begins from an access road about 100 metres north of the Beaver Creek Campground. Four kilometres into the climb, the forest gives way to Horseshoe Canyon Viewpoint—which can also be reached by car—offering spectacular vistas to the north and northwest. At dusk, the lights of Medicine Hat shimmer some seventy kilometres in the distance. Wildflowers carpet the plateau in the spring and early summer, rivaling the best displays of the Rocky Mountain foothills.

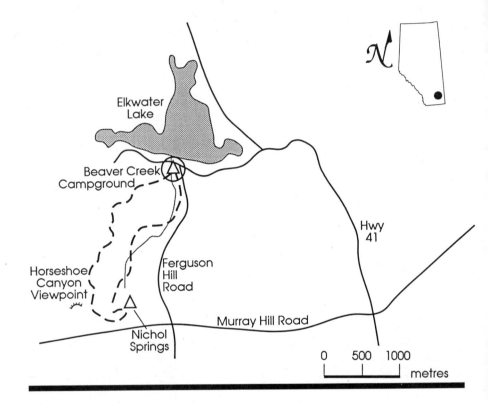

From the viewpoint, a footpath cuts east for one kilometre through an aspen and lodgepole pine forest, leading to Nichol Springs Campground. Look for spotted and striped coralroot, pinedrops, and rattlesnake plantain in the undergrowth and nuthatches and dark-eyed juncos flitting between trees in this mature forest. The campground offers ten tent sites with a picnic shelter, toilets, fire pits, and a natural spring for drinking water. The spring is reputed to supply the best water in the region, but park officials recommend boiling or filtering before drinking it. The walk-in campground is used primarily by motorists who park 200 metres away along the Murray Hill Road.

To complete the loop, take the Beaver Creek trail back to Elkwater, leaving Nichol Springs from the northwest end of the campground near site number ten. The trail proceeds downhill for three kilometres in a dense spruce forest and past several beaver ponds, with some wet footing as the trail follows Beaver Creek. The trail ends at the southwest corner of the Beaver Creek Campground. Strong hikers can walk this eight-kilometre loop in half a day, but it is wise to set aside some time for taking in the scenery and woodland flora and fauna.—*Keith Bocking*

Looking north across the Cypress Hills plateau.

HIKE 44 *HILLSIDE*

General description: A short but steep stroll to a viewpoint above Reesor Lake and the surrounding countryside.

General location: Near the Saskatchewan border in the eastern end of Cypress Hills Provincial Park.

Maps: Cypress Hills Provincial Park trail brochure; 72 E/9.

Special attractions: Views from atop the Cypress Hills Plateau.

For more information: Park Superintendent, Cypress Hills Provincial Park, Elkwater, Alberta, TOJ 1CO. Ph: (403) 893-3833.

Finding the trailhead: From Elkwater, drive five kilometres south on Highway 41 to the junction with the Reesor Lake Road. Turn left (east) and drive fifteen kilometres to the east end of Reesor Lake. Turn right onto the causeway and park in the lot on the righthand side of the road. The trail climbs immediately from the west end of the parking area.

The hike: The Hillside trail is short—only two kilometres roundtrip—but steep and rewards hikers with grand views of Reesor Lake and the surrounding countryside. Campers staying at the Reesor Lake Campground are often drawn to this hilltop in the evening to watch the play of sunset on the hills. Be sure to carry a water bottle and binoculars or a camera.

The trail is direct, a steady climb through open stands of spruce to the more open plateau on top. Views broaden with each step, first revealing the length of Reesor Lake, then encompassing neighboring hills, and finally offering glimpses of the distant prairie. The Hillside Trail provides a good vantage point for studying the local geology. An ancient, inland sea once covered this corner of Alberta, depositing layers of silt and sediments. Mighty rivers later added sediments, and these deposits proved more resistant to erosion than the surrounding land. When continental glaciers buried the plains, they ground away at the north face of the hills but the top of the plateau remained above the ice sheet.

The overlook on top is one kilometre from the trailhead, but several informal paths and game trails wander across the plateau to the south and west. Watch for white-tailed deer and elk, and some of the over-200 species of birds found in the park.

The Reesor Lake Campground contains thirty-three pull-in sites and seven walk-in tent sites. Firewood and a picnic shelter are available. Boats with electric motors are permitted on the lake and the fishing—for rainbow trout—is fair.

HIKE 44 *HILLSIDE*

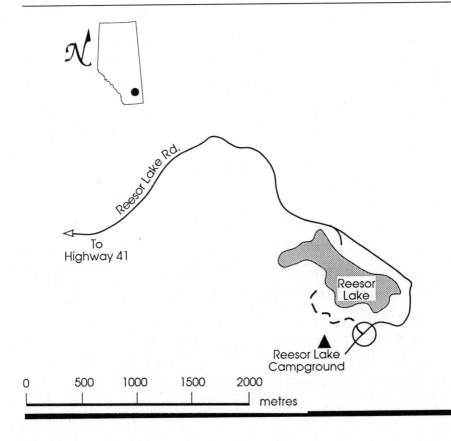

Waterton Lakes National Park

Waterton Lakes is a hikers park, a compact but diverse landscape of golden foothills, white-capped lakes, and glaciated peaks. The park also shares a border with Glacier National Park in the United States, and the two were declared an international peace park in 1932.

The 183 kilometres of trails here are well-developed and most routes are heavily travelled. July and August are the busiest months; some lower elevation trails are open in June, and sporadic good weather may lure hikers onto trails through early October. Good day hikes are found around every corner, and a handful of loop trails provide access for backpackers to some of the most spectacular alpine scenery in the Canadian Rockies.

Waterton is a wilderness park, home to black and grizzly bears, elk, moose, bighorn sheep, and mountain goats. Wildflowers are profuse, and huckleberry season (late August) rewards the slow hiker most of all. Any trip to Waterton Lakes National Park, whether a weekend outing or a two-week holiday, will provide many happy memories of trails followed and mountains climbed.

For a general map of the park and additional information, write to Park Superintendent, Waterton Lakes National Park, Waterton Park, Alberta, TOK 2MO.

HIKE 45 BEAR'S HUMP

General description: A strenuous but short walk to a vertiginous viewpoint above Waterton Townsite.

General location: Waterton Townsite, Waterton Lakes National Park in southwestern Alberta.

Maps: Waterton Lakes National Park.

Special attractions: Spectacular views, photography opportunities, wildlife.

For more information: Park Superintendent, Waterton Lakes National Park, Waterton Park, Alberta, TOK 2MO. Ph: (403) 859-2224.

Finding the trailhead: The trail begins at the Information Centre directly across from the access road to the Prince of Wales Hotel. The centre can also be reached on foot from town by following the Town Bypass Trail north from Cameron Falls.

The hike: The massive glacier that carved the Waterton Valley also chewed through a solid rock wall which once connected Mount Crandell with Vimy Peak to the southeast. The Bear's Hump, an outcrop of scoured bedrock rising above the Waterton Townsite, is the remnant of that wall. From atop

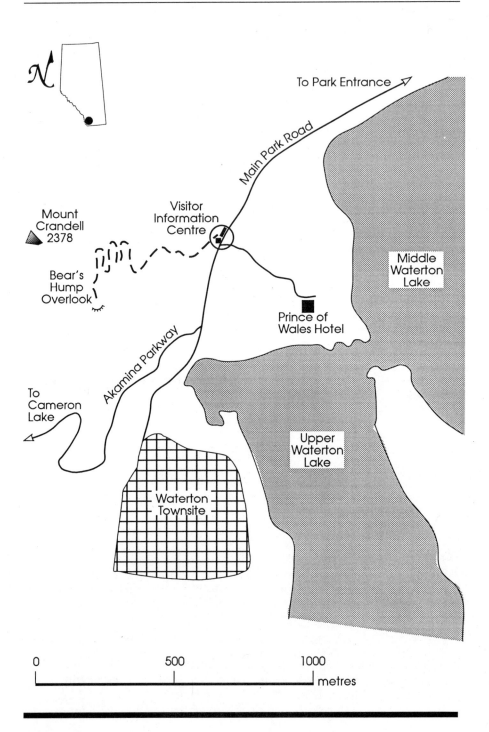

N

To Park Entrance →

Main Park Road

Mount
Crandell
2378

Visitor
Information
Centre

Bear's
Hump
Overlook

Middle
Waterton
Lake

Akamina Parkway

Prince of
Wales Hotel

To
Cameron
Lake

Upper
Waterton
Lake

Waterton
Townsite

0   500   1000
metres

the Hump, hiker's are rewarded with a dizzying view of the town and Waterton Lakes, with mountain peaks and ridges shimmering to the south and the prairie rolling away to the north and east. The panorama is best enjoyed at sunrise, but is well worth the effort during any hour of the day.

Be forewarned: the trail climbs over 200 metres in one kilometre. After the initial approach, the trail to the top spirals like a staircase in a series of square-timber steps ingenuously pinned to the mountainside. The forest covering is rather thin and the Hump can be a hot trudge during mid day.

Once on the Bear's Hump Trail, stay on the path—the hillside soil is fragile and readily susceptible to erosion. In particular, do not cut switchbacks.

The summit is reached after one final knee-weakening push, and you'll want to catch your breath before venturing onto the rocky knob, which falls away rather abruptly (and can be slippery when wet). Don't throw anything over the edge. Climbers sometimes scale the rock face, and the Akamina Parkway runs directly below the cliff. Keep a watchful eye—or better yet, a tight grip—on children.

For those with strength left in their legs, the rocky ridge angling up toward Mount Crandell offers some interesting scrambling. Take care to avoid loosening rocks onto hikers below, and keep an eye out for bighorn sheep on the less accessible walls above.

HIKE 46 *BERTHA LAKE*

General description: A moderate day hike or overnight to a beautiful cirque lake.

General location: Just south of the Waterton Townsite in Waterton Lakes National Park.

Maps: Waterton Lakes National Park.

Special attractions: Views of Upper Waterton Lake, Upper and Lower Bertha Falls, wildlife, and camping at Bertha Lake.

For more information: Park Superintendent, Waterton Lakes National Park, Waterton Park, Alberta, TOK 2MO. Ph: (403) 859-2224.

Finding the trailhead: To get to the trailhead, follow Evergreen Avenue to the southwest end of the Waterton Townsite. About 200 metres past Cameron Falls and just before the cul de sac at Cameron Bay, turn right into the gravel parking lot. A sign marks the trailhead at the south end of the lot.

The hike: The trail to Bertha Lake is one the most popular hikes in Waterton Lakes National Park, and for good reason. The trail first skirts high above Upper Waterton Lake, offering spectacular views, and then winds its way up a steep-walled vale filled with wildflowers and waterfalls, finally ending at a splendid subalpine lake ringed by mountains.

The trail climbs gradually through a mixed conifer forest, crossing streams and avalanche chutes at the base of Bertha Peak. Interpretive signs explaining basic forest ecology dot the trail for the first 2.5 kilometres. Wildflowers, including glacier lilies, cow parsnip, lupine, and shooting star, are abundant, as are deer and songbirds.

About 1.5 kilometres from the trailhead a short side trail leads left to a scenic overlook above Upper Waterton Lake. Just beyond this spur, the Lakeshore Trail also drops off to the left. The trail to Bertha Lake bears right, leading across an open ledge, again offering lake views before turning west into the Bertha Creek drainage. The gradient remains easy, entering an open forest of fir and lodgepole pine high above the roaring creek. Just before Lower Bertha Falls, at 2.5 kilometres, a horse trail branches right—hikers should stay to the left to join the creek at a picnic spot near the bridge below the falls. Watch for a small grey bird, the water ouzel or "dipper," flitting and feeding in the spray of the falls.

The trail climbs more steeply from the lower falls, crossing the foot of a broad avalanche slope at the toe of Mount Richards. A series of switchbacks

The bridge below LowerBertha Falls.

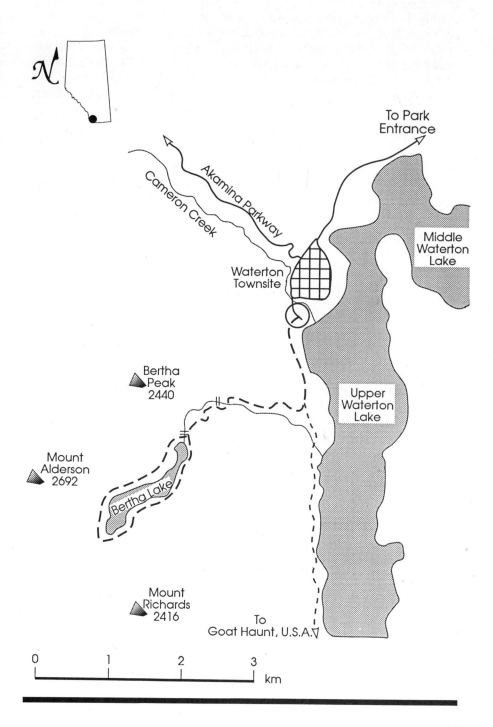

reenters the subalpine forest, contouring around the north flank of Mount Richards toward a sheer headwall that guards the Bertha Lake basin. Occasional openings allow glimpses of Upper Bertha Falls spilling over the lip of the headwall. The trail climbs to the mouth of the basin, then drops quickly down to the northeast shore of the lake, seven kilometres from the trailhead, with Mount Richards and Mount Alderson towering over the basin. The campsite is to the right on the northwest shore, and a footpath circles the entire lakeshore. Look for mountain goats and bighorn sheep on the rock walls high in the cirque.

Day hikers will need about two hours for the return trip to town. If you plan to camp overnight at Bertha Lake, obtain a backcountry permit at the Visitor Information Centre.

HIKE 47   *LAKESHORE TRAIL*

General description: A boat cruise followed by an easy day hike back to Waterton Townsite along the shores of Upper Waterton Lake.
General location: The west shore of Upper Waterton Lake in Waterton Lakes National Park.
Maps: Waterton Lakes National Park.
Special attractions: A ride on the tour boat, crossing the international boundary into Glacier National Park, Montana, wildlife, Upper Waterton Lake, mountain scenery.
For more information: Park Superintendent, Waterton Lakes National Park, Waterton Park, Alberta, TOK 2MO. Ph: (403) 859-2224. Shoreline Cruises, Box 126, Waterton, Alberta, TOK 2MO. Ph: (403) 859-2362.
Finding the trailhead: Park at the Emerald Bay Marina at the north end of Waterton Avenue in Waterton Townsite. For a reasonable fee, you can board one of the Shoreline Cruise boats, departing Waterton at 9:00 and 10:00 a.m., and 1:00 and 4:00 p.m., daily from June 30 through September 2. The cruise boats are modern, all-weather vessels operated by a private concessioner.

The hike: In 1932, the Canadian Parliament and U.S. Congress established the world's first international peace park, officially recognizing the shared natural qualities of Waterton Lakes and Glacier national parks. Though a geopolitical boundary divides the two parks, the land was shaped by the same forces and many of the same species of native plants and animals reside in both parks. Hikers in Waterton have a unique opportunity to explore both sides of the boundary by walking the Lakeshore Trail along Upper Waterton Lake.

The Upper Waterton Valley was carved by several massive glaciers moving north from what is now Glacier National Park. As the last of the glaciers receded, meltwater formed Upper Waterton Lake, at 152 metres the deepest lake in the Rocky Mountains. The Lakeshore Trail follows the western rim of this spectacular lake from the Goat Haunt Visitor Centre in

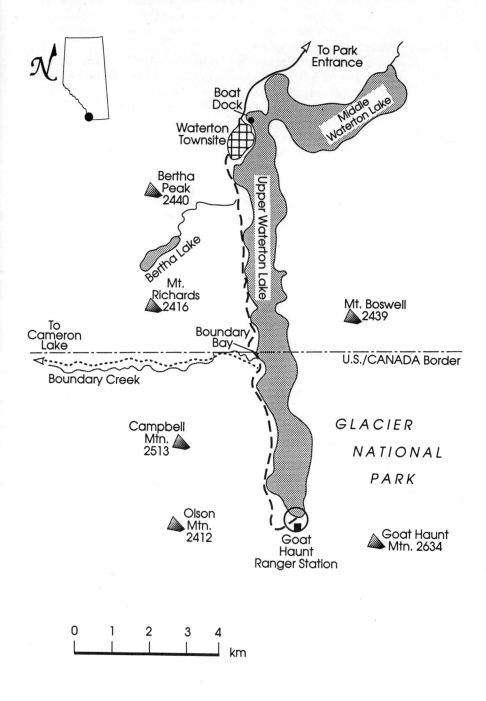

To Park
Entrance

Boat
Dock

Waterton
Townsite

Middle
Waterton Lake

Bertha
Peak
2440

Upper Waterton Lake

Bertha Lake

Mt.
Richards
2416

Mt. Boswell
2439

To
Cameron
Lake

Boundary
Bay

Boundary Creek

U.S./CANADA Border

Campbell
Mtn.
2513

GLACIER

NATIONAL

PARK

Olson
Mtn.
2412

Goat
Haunt
Ranger Station

Goat Haunt
Mtn. 2634

0   1   2   3   4
km

Glacier National Park north for eleven kilometres to Waterton Townsite.

The one-way cruise to Goat Haunt hugs the eastern shoreline and takes about an hour. The morning cruise times are best for spotting wildlife and enjoying the day's early light. Once at Goat Haunt, stop in the Visitor Centre to see the interpretive displays and consider a 1.5 kilometre side trip to Rainbow Falls on the Waterton River.

The Lakeshore Trail begins about 500 metres west of the Goat Haunt Visitor Centre. Bear right at the junction with the Rainbow Falls trail, and continue north past several trails that lead up Olson Creek to the west. Within 1.5 kilometres the Lakeshore Trail drops close to the lake's western shore, then contours evenly along the foot of Campbell Mountain.

Roughly five kilometres from Goat Haunt the North Boundary Trail breaks to the left. Continue north, across Boundary Creek to the stone cairn marking the 49th Parallel and the international boundary between Canada and the United States.

The remaining six kilometres of trail roll over the small ridges and ravines on the flank of Mount Richards, rich habitat for some of the twenty-two species of orchids found in Waterton. You can stop for lunch or fish on the lakeshore at Boundary and Bertha bays, and overnight campsites are provided at Boundary Bay for hikers with backcountry permits.

From the water's edge at Bertha Bay the trail climbs abruptly to the junction with the Bertha Lake Trail. Turn right at this junction and continue north 1.5 kilometres to the Bertha Lake trailhead and parking lot at the southwest corner of the Waterton Townsite. Aim for the footbridge over Cameron Creek, then skirt the campground to reach Waterton Avenue and the Emerald Bay Marina.

HIKE 48 *CRANDELL LAKE*

General description: An easy day hike to a small tree-lined mountain lake.
General location: Northwest of the Waterton Townsite, roughly in the centre of Waterton Lakes National Park.
Maps: Waterton Lakes National Park.
Special attractions: Crandell Lake, wildflowers, views of the lower Blakiston Valley.
For more information: Park Superintendent, Waterton Lakes National Park, Waterton Park, Alberta, T0K 2M0. Ph: (403) 859-2224.
Finding the trailhead: The shortest of the three approaches to the lake begins on the Akamina Parkway about seven kilometres west of the Waterton Townsite. Look for a pullout on the north side of the road, often crowded with cars. This trail follows an old road grade for the first 800 metres, gently but steadily climbing to a junction with the Crandell Lake Loop Trail. From here, the trail drops quickly to the lake in another 400 metres.

The hike: Crandell Lake is scenic woodland pool set in the rock benches between Mount Crandell and Ruby Ridge. Only one kilometre north of the

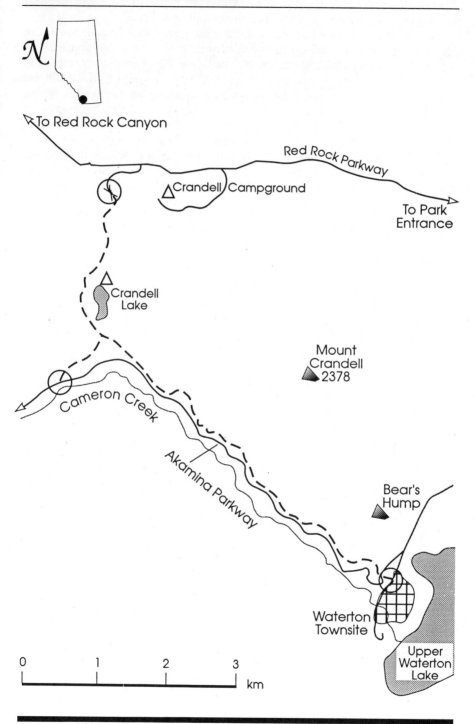

To Red Rock Canyon

Red Rock Parkway

Crandell Campground

To Park Entrance

Crandell Lake

Mount Crandell 2378

Cameron Creek

Akamina Parkway

Bear's Hump

Waterton Townsite

Upper Waterton Lake

0   1   2   3   km

Akamina Parkway, Crandell is one of the most accessible of Waterton's backcountry lakes and is a popular destination for families and casual hikers. But two other approaches to Crandell Lake offer longer hikes for those who believe getting there is at least half of the fun.

A more inviting hike beckons from the Blakiston Valley side, beginning just west of the Crandell Mountain Campground, which lies about seven kilometres up the Red Rock Parkway. Those staying at the campground can walk west along the camp access road (past the closure gate) to the trailhead. Day visitors should drive one kilometre past the campground entrance on the Red Rock Parkway to the Canyon Camp access road. The highway sign here also mentions Crandell Lake. Park in the grassy area above Blakiston Creek and walk across the bridge, bearing southeast to the trail sign.

This 2.5-kilometre trail climbs a series of rock benches, following an old wagon road. The path is wide, gently graded, and usually sheltered from Waterton's winds. Wildflowers are abundant and there are good views of Mount Galwey to the north.

The third and longest approach to Crandell Lake begins in the town of Waterton, providing a good early season hike at low elevation. From the townsite campground, walk west along Cameron Creek to the Townsite Bypass Trail at Cameron Falls. Head north for a few hundred metres to the junction with the Crandell Lake Trail, branching west and uphill. This junction can also be reached from the information centre north of town by climbing the stairs above the parking lot and dropping south along the Bypass Trail, across the Akamina Parkway, and behind the townsite for several hundred metres.

The main trail immediately crosses the Akamina Parkway, then climbs

Bighorn sheep, like these full-curl rams, are a common sight in Waterton's front country.

sharply above the road for one kilometre. The grade eases off as the trail contours around the flanks of Mount Crandell, sometimes cutting through the limestone cliff and passing small waterfalls. The pass above Crandell Lake is reached in 6.5 kilometres, joining the short trail down to the Akamina Parkway. The main trail continues another four kilometres downhill to the lake.

Hikers using any of these three trails are advised to wear running shoes or similar footwear, which do less damage to the soil than lug-soled hiking boots. As always, stay on the trail and avoid trampling the vegetation in this heavily-used area.

HIKE 49 *LINEHAM FALLS*

General description: An easy day hike to a 100-metre waterfall in a little-visited drainage.
General location: Near Mount Blakiston and the western boundary of Waterton Lakes National Park.
Maps: Waterton Lakes National Park.
Special attractions: Lineham Falls, wildlife, mountain scenery, and an uncrowded trail.
For more information: Park Superintendent, Waterton Lakes National Park, Waterton Park, Alberta, TOK 2MO. Ph: (403) 859-2224.
Finding the trailhead: After entering Waterton Lakes National Park on Highway 5, turn right onto the Akamina Parkway just before entering the Waterton Townsite. Follow the parkway along the Cameron Valley for about nine kilometres. The trail begins at an unmarked pullout on the right one kilometre past the historic marker for the first oil well in western Canada. If you pass the marked trailhead for Rowe Lakes, you've driven too far.

The hike: The Lineham Creek drainage is less visited than most of Waterton's accessible valleys, primarily because a 100-metre cliff prevents all but skilled climbers from reaching the chain of lakes in the upper basin. But the lower valley offers its own rewards for less daring hikers.

The Lineham Creek trail sign is found 100 metres up the trail, along with a warning about the hazards of scaling the cliff at the head of the drainage. Experienced climbers with the proper equipment may attempt the cliff, but they must first register with a park ranger at the administration office in town.

The trail climbs quickly out of the forest and onto an open, grassy slope with good views of 2,728 Mount Lineham to the southwest. After two kilometres the grade eases and a subalpine forest shades the trail. The view opens again in another 1.5 kilometres, with mounts Lineham and Blakiston framing the white strand of Lineham Creek as it plummets over the headwall

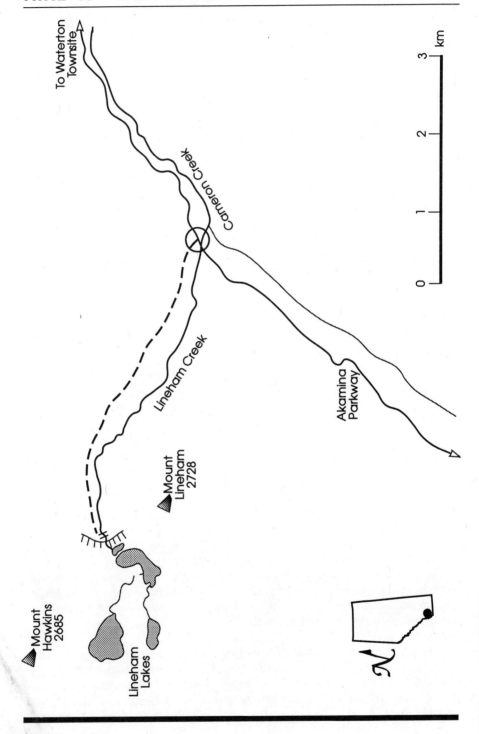

to the lower valley, 100 metres below.

From here, the trail dips and climbs slightly for another kilometre to the base of the cliff, roughly four kilometres from the trailhead. This is a good spot for lunch and a long look at the cliff and adjacent slopes, watching for mountain goats and bighorn sheep.

HIKE 50 *UPPER ROWE LAKES*

General description: A moderate day hike or overnighter to a pair of high subalpine lakes.
General location: On the western boundary of Waterton Lakes National Park.
Maps: Waterton Lakes National Park.
Special attractions: Upper and Lower Rowe Lakes, a variety of subalpine plant communities, wildlife.
For more information: Park Superintendent, Waterton Lakes National Park, Waterton Park, Alberta, TOK 2MO. Ph: (403) 859-2224.
Finding the trailhead: From Waterton townsite drive eleven kilometres up the Akamina Parkway to a small gravel parking area on the righthand side of the road. A sign marks the trailhead at the far end of the parking lot.

The hike: The six-kilometre trail to Upper Rowe Lakes is one of the most scenic in Waterton, and also one of the more gradual climbs to timberline. The trail follows an easy grade for all but the final kilometre, and there are several appealing destinations along the way for those interested in a shorter day hike. Rowe Meadow offers backpackers a pleasant site for a base camp or an overnight on the way up the Tamarack Trail.

Initially, the trail parallels Rowe Creek, offering glimpses of the noisy stream as it tumbles over the brilliant red bedrock. After 300 metres, the trail breaks away from the creek in a pair of broad, gentle switchbacks.

Many hikers climb above the switchbacks as the trail ascends the ridge between Rowe and Lineham creeks, but the views here are disappointing. Refrain from adding your footprints to the fragile soil by keeping to the trail as you climb. Wildflowers are profuse through this section, with paintbrush, lupine, phlox, and aster thriving in the mosaic of shade and sun that patterns the ridge. Deer also frequent the trail, feeding on the lush vegetation.

Over the next four kilometres the trail contours gradually up the lower flank of Mount Lineham, moving through open avalanche corridors and stands of spruce and fir. Watch for thimbleberries and huckleberries in August. After passing closer to the creek, a short side trail drops across the creek to the left and then climbs to Lower Rowe Lake, a good site for a rest stop or a suitable destination for casual hikers.

The main trail continues for another kilometre to Rowe Meadow and the designated campsite. The trail forks at the far side of the meadow just after crossing a small stream, the right fork leading to the Tamarack Trail and the left fork to Upper Rowe Lakes. The trail to the upper basin climbs a set of steep switchbacks and then levels off before reaching the lakes, about 1.5 kilometres and 200 vertical metres from Rowe Meadow. The uppermost lake is also the largest, surrounded by the talus slopes of Mount Rowe and a scattering of fir and alpine larch.

A side trail leads down to the middle lake, a small tarn surrounded by plates of shale. Follow the outlet stream bed to the overhanging headwall for a vertiginous view of Lower Rowe Lake and the Cameron Valley beyond.

For those who want to explore the Lineham Lakes basin but are stifled by the 100-metre cliff at the head of Lineham Creek (see hike 49), an alternate

Upper Rowe Lake in Waterton National Park.

route lies over Tamarack Pass. This byway should be attempted only by hikers in excellent physical shape who are well versed in mountain travel and route-finding. Take a topo map, wear sturdy shoes, and wait for fair weather. From Rowe Meadow, climb the scree slopes to the pass, and then contour north along the ridge above Lineham Lakes. A faint, unofficial trail, originally a goat path, descends the scree slide below Mount Hawkins to the lake basin. This route is the only way back out of the basin. See a park ranger for more information.

HIKE 50   *UPPER ROWE LAKES*

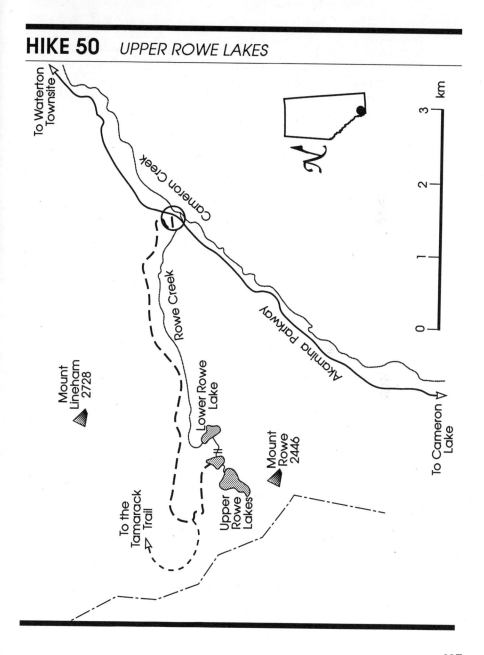

HIKE 51 CARTHEW PASS

General description: A moderate day hike to a high alpine pass overlooking the remote northern mountains of Glacier National Park in the United States.
General location: East of Cameron Lake near the southern boundary of Waterton Lakes National Park.
Maps: Waterton Lakes National Park.
Special attractions: Cameron Lake, Summit Lake, approach to Mount Carthew's summit, spectacular mountain scenery, wildlife.
For more information: Park Superintendent, Waterton Lakes National Park, Waterton Park, Alberta, TOK 2MO. Ph: (403) 859-2224.
Finding the trailhead: From Waterton townsite, drive west sixteen kilometres on the Akamina Parkway to the Cameron Lake parking lot at the end of the road. Follow the lakeshore trail to the left past the boat rental concession to the bridge over Cameron Creek. The trail to Summit Lake and Carthew Pass begins here.

The hike: From the forested shore of Cameron Lake to the blustery, barren summit of Mount Carthew, this hike is packed with mountain lakes, wildflowers, panoramic views, berry patches, glimpses of glaciers, and wildlife. Many day hikers on this trail venture no further than Summit Lake, but those who go the extra distance to Carthew Pass will find it well worth the effort. Be sure to carry plenty of drinking water (do not drink from Summit Lake without first boiling or purifying the water), and pack along a raincoat and a warm sweater.

The route to Carthew Pass.

From Cameron Lake, the trail rises gradually through a 300-year-old forest of spruce and fir in a series of long, gentle switchbacks. Watch for the pale turquoise of Cameron Lake peeking through occasional breaks in the forest canopy, and keep an eye to the trailside foliage for thimbleberries and huckleberries in season.

After climbing for three kilometres, the trail levels and dips slightly to the north shore of Summit Lake some four kilometres from the trailhead. Most hikers stop here for lunch, but an earlier start allows those more adventurous to continue hiking up to Carthew Pass, four kilometres distant. Turn left at

HIKE 51   *CARTHEW PASS*

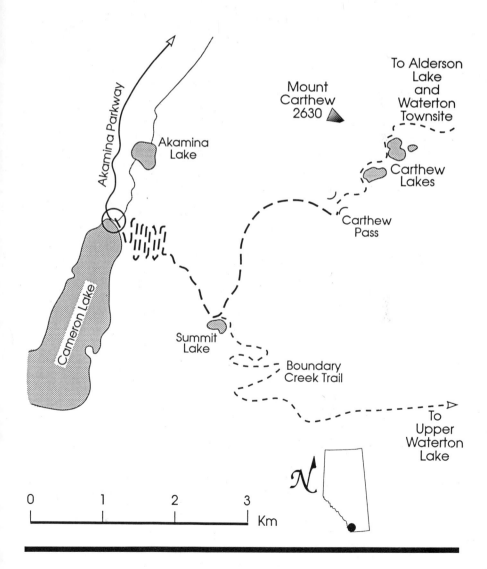

the trail junction just above Summit Lake and climb over the low spur into a wide subalpine basin. The trail crosses below a broken rock band frequented by bighorn sheep then sweeps across the southern arm of Mount Carthew at timberline.

As you climb above stands of stunted fir, larch, and whitebark pine, the southern horizon opens to reveal glaciers hugging the walls of Mount Custer and Chapman Peak, with lakes Nooney and Wurdeman cupped in their respective cirques. The trail ends its long contour by zig-zagging steeply up a red scree slope to the pass at 2,300 metres. The pass, and the summit beyond, should be attempted only during fair weather and with plenty of daylight remaining. The ridge offers no shelter from wind, rain, or lightning, and storms brew quickly in this region.

For even more spectacular views, hikers can climb the spur leading north from the saddle to the summit ridge of Mount Carthew. The peak itself lies one kilometre north along this barren ridge and offers a 360-degree panorama of mountains, glaciers, and glistening lakes. Total distance from the trailhead to the summit is just under ten kilometres; allow about four hours for the one-way trip.

HIKE 52 *ALDERSON LAKE*

General description: A strenuous day hike or moderate overnighter that takes the hiker through old-growth forest and subalpine berry patches, over a high alpine pass with spectacular views, and down to the shores of a handful of beautiful lakes.

General location: Southwest of the Waterton townsite in Waterton National Park.

Maps: Waterton Lakes National Park.

Special attractions: Numerous lakes, fishing, wildflowers, an alpine pass, dense forests, and spectacular mountain scenery.

For more information: Park Superintendent, Waterton Lakes National Park, Waterton Park, Alberta, TOK 2MO. Ph: (403) 859-2224.

Finding the trailhead: From Waterton townsite, drive west sixteen kilometres on the Akamina Parkway to the Cameron Lake parking lot at the end of the road. Follow the lakeshore trail to the left past the boat rental concession to the bridge over Cameron Creek. The trail to Summit Lake, Carthew Pass, and Alderson Lake begins here.

The hike: Few hikes in the Canadian Rockies can match this one for the variety of terrain and ecological communities encountered. The well-graded trail traverses old-growth forest, subalpine lakeshores, vast huckleberry patches, a windswept alpine pass, snowfields, and a riparian corridor. Much of the middle section of trail runs at or above timberline with excellent views of distant peaks and lakes, and observant hikers may see mule deer, bighorn sheep, mountain goats, and the occasional bear.

HIKE 52 *ALDERSON LAKE*

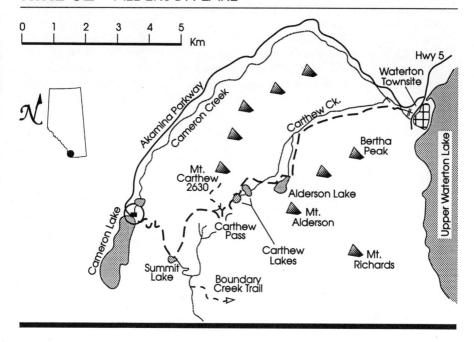

The trail quickly leaves the northeast shore of Cameron Lake in a series of broad, easy switchbacks through old-growth spruce and fir. There are glimpses of Cameron Lake and Forum Peak through the trees, and the blooms of Indian paintbrush, cow parsnip, aster, and glacier lily line the way.

After climbing for three kilometres, the trail levels off and angles to the southwest through a dense huckleberry thicket and a scattered stand of alpine larch. A slight downgrade brings you to Summit Lake and the junction with the Boundary Creek and Carthew Pass trails, about four kilometres from the Cameron Lake trailhead. Turn left and follow the Carthew-Alderson trail as it climbs into a broad basin hanging above Boundary Creek.

Here the trail contours neatly along the southern arm of 2,630-metre Mount Carthew, gradually rising out of the scattered larch and white-bark pine to switchback abruptly up the red argillite scree slope onto Carthew Pass. The pass, at 2,300 metres, offers splendid views into a remote corner of Glacier National Park in the United States. Mount Custer and Chapman Peak soar above the Herbst and Hudson glaciers, which in turn feed lakes Nooney and Wurdeman below.

If the weather is clear, the summit of Mount Carthew is well worth a detour from the trail. Drop your packs on the saddle and follow the slope northwest onto the long summit ridge, turning north to climb one kilometre to the peak. The vistas here include Cameron Lake, Akamina Pass, and

Mount Rowe to the west, Buchanan Ridge to the north, Carthew Lakes and Mount Alderson to the east, and even better views of Glacier Park's northern ranges to the south.

From the pass, the trail drops quickly to a narrow, rocky draw containing the two Carthew Lakes. Snowfields often linger here well into mid-summer—use caution on the steep sections, kicking in steps if necessary. The trail skirts the west shores of both lakes and a small cascade separating the two and reenters the forest as it crosses several rockbands on the descent to Alderson Lake. The designated campsites are found at the far end of the lake below the sheer north face of 2,692-metre Mount Alderson. The campground is thirteen kilometres from Cameron Lake and nearly seven kilometres from the end of the trail in Waterton Townsite.

After fishing for cutthroat trout or just contemplating the emerald waters of Alderson Lake for an evening, hikers continue down the trail along Carthew Creek. The trail stays east of the creek, contouring steadily down the drainage to its confluence with Cameron Creek, then rounding the flank of Bertha Peak to the trailhead on Evergreen Avenue just below Cameron Falls.

Most hikers arrange a ride back to Cameron Lake to pick up their car, but the sporting goods store in Waterton's Tamarack Mall offers a shuttle service up the Akamina Parkway, eliminating the need to leave a car at the trailhead.

The trail to Alderson Lake offers spectacular scenery including vistas of north Glacier National Park.

HIKE 53 *GOAT LAKE*

General description: An arduous day hike or overnight to a high alpine lake.
General location: Near the northwestern boundary of Waterton Lakes National Park.
Maps: Waterton Lakes National Park.
Special attractions: Rugged mountain scenery, Goat Lake, fishing, mountain goats, wildlife.
For more information: Park Superintendent, Waterton Lakes National Park, Waterton Park, Alberta, TOK 2MO. Ph: (403) 859-2224.
Finding the trailhead: The hike begins at the end of the Red Rock Parkway fourteen kilometres from the junction with the park's main entrance road.

Goat Lake gets its name from the mountain goats that scramble on the cliffs above the lake.

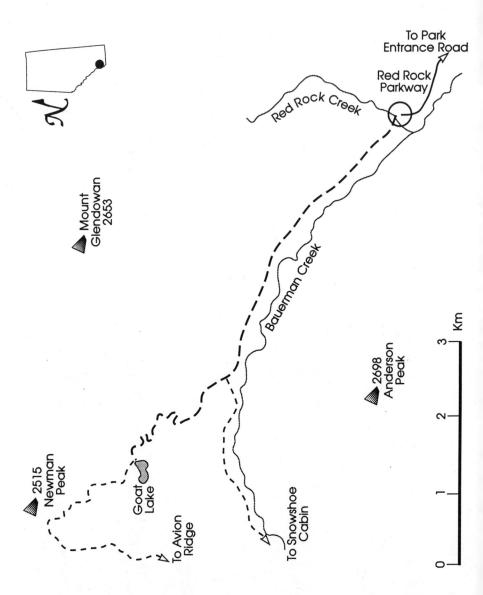

From the loop parking lot, cross the bridge over Red Rock Creek and head west on the Snowshoe Trail along Bauerman Creek.

The hike: The trip to Goat Lake is for many hikers the epitome of the Waterton backcountry experience: a steep, arduous ascent; few other hikers; alpine meadows studded with wildflowers; and a gem of a lake set against sheer stone walls. The designated campsite on the west shore of the lake serves well as a base camp for exploring the basin and the surrounding ridges. If you're dayhiking, allow a full day for the fourteen-kilometre roundtrip.

The Snowshoe Trail is an old service road leading to the Snowshoe patrol cabin near the head of Bauerman Creek. The trail is wide and flat, gaining less than fifty metres in elevation over the first 4.5 kilometres.

At this point, the trail to Goat Lake takes off to the right at a heart-pounding gradient and never eases off. Much of the route traverses an open south-facing slope that can be scorching on a sunny summer day. Carry plenty of water and adjust your pace accordingly.

As it approaches the upper basin, the trail switchbacks above the creek cascading down the headwall. Look for bright red monkeyflowers and the busy water ouzel at the water's edge. At seven kilometres the trail meets the lake's shoreline. The campsite is 100 metres to the west, with glimpses of the lake and the ridge above. Goat Lake was named for the mountain goats that frequent these rock walls. The basin also supports a healthy population of ground squirrels, an ample food source for the resident grizzly bear and golden eagles.

Anglers can stalk the small but abundant cutthroat trout in Goat Lake, while hikers with energy to spare after the trek in may want to explore the ridge running from 2,515-metre Newman Peak to the northwest. A path leads from the campsite up the left side of the basin, then snakes around a set of cliffs to gain the upper scree slopes. Use care on the loose rocks and be mindful of other hikers above or below. A faint trail follows the crest of the ridge leading north around the horn of Newman Peak into the Yarrow Creek basin, or south to Avion Ridge and the headwaters of Bauerman Creek (see Hike #54 –the Avion Ridge Loop).

HIKE 54   *AVION RIDGE*

General description: A strenuous but highly scenic two- or three-day trek through a remote corner of Waterton's high country.
General location: Along the northwest boundary of Waterton Lakes National Park.
Maps: Waterton Lakes National Park.
Special attractions: Spectacular views from 2,300-metre Avion Ridge, Lost Lake, Goat Lake, mountain goats, bighorn sheep.
For more information: Park Superintendent, Waterton Lakes National Park, Waterton Park, Alberta, T0K 2M0. Ph: (403) 859-2224.

HIKE 54 AVION RIDGE

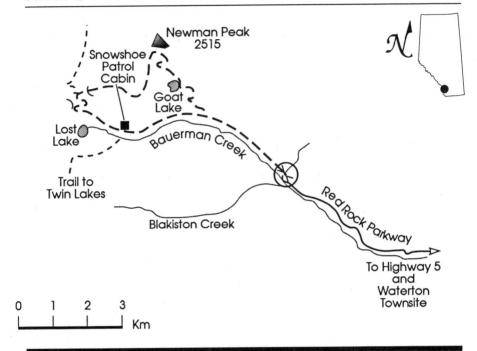

Finding the trailhead: From the main park road, turn west onto the Red Rock Parkway and drive fourteen kilometres to the parking lot at the end of the road. Walk across the bridge above Red Rock Creek and continue straight ahead, following the Snowshoe Trail, an abandoned service road.

The hike: Avion Ridge offers one of the longest unbroken stretches of high-elevation hiking within Waterton Lakes National Park. The ridgeline, over four kilometres of trail above timberline, is a narrow, scree-covered spine that seems to soar above the distant horizons. Rows of mountains rise in all directions and golden eagles ride the waves of wind that spill over the divide. From the ridge, hikers are likely to look down upon mountain goats, bighorn sheep, and deer on lower slopes.

These rewards make the long, tedious approach worthwhile, and hikers can take some solace in the knowledge that the first eight kilometres along the Snowshoe Trail are nearly flat, gaining just over 200 metres in elevation. Take note of the Goat Lake trail at the four-kilometre mark; this route serves as the last leg of the Avion Ridge loop. The service road is open to mountain bike travel as far as the Snowshoe Cabin, offering a much faster approach to the high country for those so inclined.

Plan to spend the first night at the Snowshoe Campground near the trail junction at the end of the Snowshoe Trail. Get an early start on the second day, unless the weather is threatening. Don't attempt the ridgeline hike if visibility is poor or foul weather is brewing; the trail is indistinct much of the

136

Avion Ridge in Waterton Lakes National Park.

way and there is no shelter from lightning, wind, and rain once on the ridge.

To reach Avion Ridge, turn right at the Snowshoe junction and begin the steady climb to the Castle River Divide. This 2,000- metre pass is reached in three kilometres, with a short set of switchbacks cutting more steeply at the end. Follow the rising ridge to the east, watching for the lightly-worn track as you wander through an open glade of alpine larch. Stay atop the ridge and continue eastward for slightly over two kilometres, using goat trails where the official tread is too thin to follow. As the route drops from the apex of Avion Ridge it turns to the north, crosses a high saddle, and climbs again to a rocky prominence guarding the view into the Goat Lake basin. The most obvious track here clings to the western face of the outcrop, exposed to the brunt of prevailing winds and falling away to the headwaters of the Castle River far below.

Immediately after rounding the outcrop look for a trail sign for Goat Lake. An obvious trail descends on scree to the right, zig-zagging across the upper basin wall. The path threads between several rocky bands and broken cliffs, occasionally braiding around clumps of small trees and through boulder fields. Look for cairns and favour any leads to your left as you descend (see also Hike # 53–Goat Lake).

A final leg of the switchbacks leads to a trickle of a stream, and then jogs to the left through a band of trees and down a final rock ledge. From here to the lake be alert for bear sign and make noise when moving through dense cover or along the noisy stream. The Goat Lake basin is home to at least one grizzly bear nearly every year, and though confrontations are rare, a surprise would be unpleasant. Below the ledge the trail meets the true timberline, crosses a rough gully to the opposite side of the basin, and cuts through a grove of fir stunted and deformed by frequent avalanches. The trail here is well defined and runs through a lush meadow to the campsites on the north shore of Goat Lake.

Plan to camp here at least one night, or two to better enjoy the fishing, goat-watching, and peace and quiet. The campsites and lakeshore are in good condition, evidence of low use and conscientious campers. Be sure to leave the area as clean and untrampled as you found it.

On the final day, follow the trail around the east end of Goat Lake and along the outlet stream to the lip of the headwall above Bauerman Creek. The trail drops quickly in a few broad switchbacks across open rock slopes, then moderates as it enters the forest. The junction with the Snowshoe Trail lies 2.5 kilometres from Goat Lake. Turn left and follow the old service road back to the trailhead.

The total length of this hike is twenty-three kilometres, though most hikers will nearly double this distance by adding a visit to Lost Lake on their way up to the Castle River Divide and roaming around the various spurs and upper slopes adjoining Avion Ridge. And an obvious route climbs Newman Peak, a 2,515-metre peak to the north of Goat Lake, from the trail sign on the saddle.

Bow-Crow Forest

HIKE 55 *CROWSNEST MOUNTAIN*

General description: A strenuous day hike to the top of Crowsnest Mountain, one of the finest viewpoints in the Canadian Rockies.
General location: North of Crowsnest Pass in southern Alberta where Highway 3 crosses the Continental Divide into British Columbia.
Maps: 82 G/10.
Special attractions: Excellent views in all directions from atop Crowsnest Mountain.
For more information: Bow-Crow Forest, 8660 Bearspaw Dam Road Northwest, Calgary, Alberta, T2M 4L8. Ph: (403) 297-6261.
Finding the trailhead: From the town of Coleman, drive west three kilometres on Highway 3 to the Allison Creek Road. Turn north on this paved road and drive 2.5 kilometres to a fork in the road. The left fork leads to a lakeside campground operated by the Alberta Forest Service (sites are in a lodgepole pine forest and the lake offers good fishing for rainbow trout). Take the right fork—a gravel road—to reach the hiking trail, driving just under seven kilometres to the trailhead sign. Continue past the sign another 300 metres to a narrow road and parking area on the right.

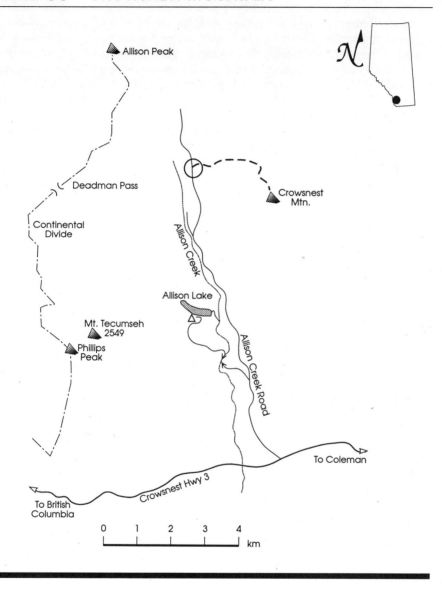

The hike: Crowsnest Mountain is a 2,804 metre pyramid of history turned upside down. The mountain was formed by a violent upheaval along the Lewis thrust fault, which folded the older Paleozoic rock on top of the younger Mesozoic formations. Today this geologic anomaly rewards determined hikers with commanding views of Alberta's rugged backbone, the Canadian Rockies.

Plan a full day for the twelve-kilometre roundtrip to the summit and back, and wait for fair weather. Pack along a sweater and windbreaker or raincoat, and carry plenty of drinking water. The trail begins with a steady climb through a second growth pine forest, an area once thinned by fire and logging. The track is well-defined and offers glimpses of the mountain through the trees until timberline is reached at the four-kilometre mark.

From timberline, the route traverses a steep scree slope to the base of massive limestone cliffs. Follow a series of cairns to a broad cleft or chimney in the cliffs. Here the trail becomes an arduous scramble up the rocky debris within the chimney, finally opening onto the gentle terraces of the upper slopes. The summit route contours directly to the top over loose shingle-like stones.

Stunning panoramic views greet the successful hiker, with Tornado Mountain dominating the northern horizon. To the west lies Deadman Pass, a low gap on the Continental Divide between 2,644 metre Allison Peak to the north and 2,549-metre Mount Tecumseh to the south. Retrace your steps to return to the trailhead. —*Peter Allen*

Crowsnest Mountain stands alone, an outlyer from the peaks of the Continental Divide. A 360-degree view awaits hikers on the summit. Peter Allen photo

140

Kananaskis Country

In 1977, the Alberta government designated Kananaskis Country as a provincial recreation area set aside primarily for Albertans. Banff and Jasper national parks were crowded with tourists and locals alike, but the Kananaskis had room to spare. The same holds true today, and this 4,000-square-kilometre preserve is still largely unknown outside the province.

Hiking trails abound here, many beginning on old logging or mining exploration roads that lead to more traditional foot paths through near-pristine wilderness. Wildlife is abundant and often more visible here than in the national parks. Watch for elk, deer, moose, bighorn sheep, and mountain goats. Black and grizzly bear are common, and some lucky campers hear the howl of wolves in the evenings.

Heavy winter snows keep higher trails—particularly those along the Continental Divide ranges—closed well into July of most years. Valley trails and some of the routes in the drier foothills to the east may be open from May through October. Weather is unpredictable, and hikers should be prepared for snow, rain, and wind on any day of the year. For more information, write to Kananaskis Country, 412, 1011 Glenmore Trail S.W., Calgary, Alberta, T2V 4R6.

HIKE 56   *PASQUE MOUNTAIN*

General description: A moderate day hike to a 2,500-metre ridge near the headwaters of the Oldman River.
General location: On the southern boundary of Kananaskis Country about sixty kilometres west of Nanton.
Maps: 82 J/2.
Special attractions: Outstanding vistas of the Continental Divide Range.
For more information: Kananaskis Country, Suite 412, 1011 Glenmore Trail S.W., Calgary, Alberta, T2V 4R6. Ph: (403) 297-3362.
Finding the trailhead: At Highwood Junction on Highway 40, turn south on Forestry Trunk Road 940. Drive south twelve kilometres to the bridge over Cataract Creek. Continue south another nine kilometres to a logging road on the west side of the Forestry Trunk Road and park by the sign prohibiting motorized vehicles. The trail begins on the logging road.

The hike: Forestry Trunk Road 940 provides good access to trails along the southern range of the Continental Divide, but many of these routes require a day or two of walking through heavily timbered valleys with limited views. For day hikers, The nine-kilometre trek to the summit ridge of Pasque

Mountain offers more immediate rewards—wildflowers, a good chance for solitude, and outstanding views of the peaks north and south on the divide.

From the trunk road, walk down the logging road and across Wilkinson Creek to a junction with another old road. Turn right and cross a second creek to follow the main road south for about one kilometre, bearing left at three subsequent junctions with other logging tracks. Here the main road bends west; veer left and cross the stream on the narrower track, which ends in a log-strewn cut.

HIKE 56 *PASQUE MOUNTAIN*

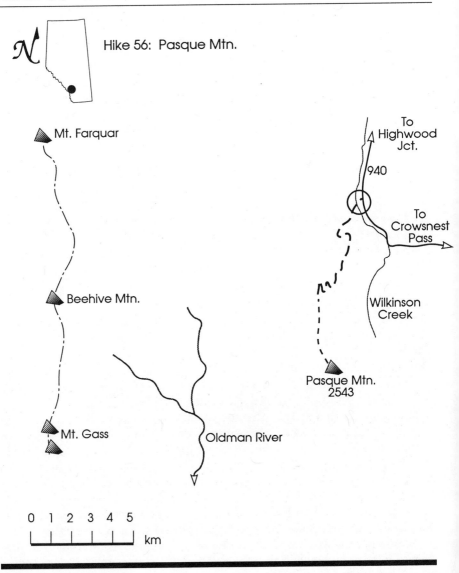

Hike 56: Pasque Mtn.

Mt. Farquar

To Highwood Jct.

940

To Crowsnest Pass

Beehive Mtn.

Wilkinson Creek

Pasque Mtn. 2543

Mt. Gass

Oldman River

0 1 2 3 4 5 km

An exploration road leaves from the uphill southern corner of the cut, climbing steadily on a spur ridge leading from the north end of Pasque Mountain. Continue from the first grassy bench as the road switchbacks more steeply up the northeast flank of the mountain, gaining broad views of Wilkinson Creek below.

The final ascent twists and turns up to a wide grassy bench. A poorly defined trail leads south to the top of the rocky, lichen-covered knob and prominent cairn on the north end of the summit ridge. Mounts Etherington, Scrimger, and Farquar line the northwest horizon and Beehive Mountain rises directly to the west. The double pyramids of Mount Gass stand to the southwest above the headwaters of the Oldman River. Look for traces of the Great Divide Trail on the east flank of Mount Gass.

If the weather is fair and your boots are sturdy, consider scrambling south along the ridge to the southern summit knob, actually the highest point on the mountain. This two-kilometre stretch is a rough walk on the narrow ridge crest, and there are two sheer, short drops requiring extra caution and judicious route-finding.

HIKE 57 *PICKLEJAR LAKES*

General description: A moderate day hike to a chain of four beautiful lakes.
General location: East of Highway 40 about fifteen kilometres south of Highwood Pass in the southern arm of Kananaskis Country.
Maps: 82 J/7, 82 J/10.
Special attractions: The four Picklejar Lakes, good views of the upper Highwood River drainage, some wildlife.
For more information: Kananaskis Country, Suite 412, 1011 Glenmore Trail S.W., Calgary, Alberta, T2V 4R6. Ph: (403) 297-3362.
Finding the trailhead: From Highwood Pass on Highway 40, drive south about fifteen kilometres to the Lantern Creek picnic area (two kilometres south of the Picklejar Creek picnic area). The picnic area and parking lot are on the west side of the road, but the trail begins on the east side just north of the picnic area and on the north bank of Lantern Creek. Look for the small trail sign at the edge of the trees.

The hike: Many hikers amble up Picklejar Creek, to the north, hoping to find Picklejar Lakes at the head of the stream. But the lakes are couched in a hanging basin, unreachable from Picklejar Creek, requiring a less obvious approach up Lantern Creek. The four lakes, each one set higher than the last, fill an elongated cirque at timberline in the Highwood Range.

Carry plenty of drinking water for the hot climb on the south-facing flanks of the Highwood Range, and also a spare shirt to change into on top, where cool breezes can raise goosebumps in the shade of the subalpine forest.

From the roadside, the trail contours gradually on the timbered north bank above Lantern Creek. Roughly two kilometres in, the trail rolls through a series of grassy swales and drops down to cross the creek, then wanders through a sparse forest. As Lantern Creek swings east, the trail angles north, recrosses the main current and climbs steadily over open slopes to a broad saddle overlooking the Picklejar drainage.

From here the trail wends down to Picklejar Creek and follows its southern bank to the first lake, just over four kilometres from the trailhead. Each lake is worth a visit. Stay on the righthand shore and follow the worn track northeast through the subalpine forest. The third and largest lake sits in a semicircle of trees and another of talus and rock slabs that slant down through the clear blue water. Look for a sunny boulder near the water's edge for a good lunch spot.

Don't give in to the temptation to follow Picklejar Creek on the way out. The gorge below the lakes is impassable and better views are found from the trail on the saddle above.

HIKE 57 *PICKLEJAR LAKES*

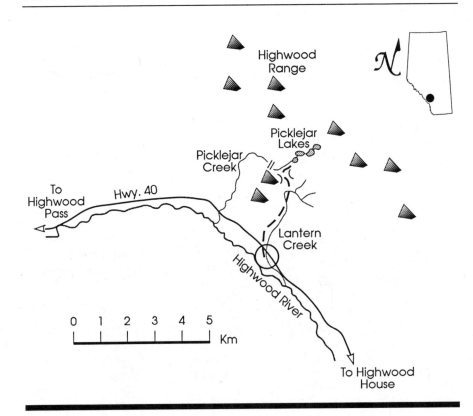

HIKE 58 *PICKLEJAR CREEK*

General description: A short day hike, bushwhacking much of the way, to an overlook above the upper Highwood River.

General location: East of Highway 40 about twelve kilometres south of Highwood Pass in Kananaskis Country.

Maps: 82 J/10.

Special attractions: Opportunities for solitude, wildlife, good views of the Highwood Range and river valley.

For more information: Kananaskis Country, Suite 412, 1011 Glenmore Trail S.W., Calgary, Alberta, T2V 4R6. Ph: (403) 297-3362.

Finding the trailhead: From Highwood Pass, drive twelve kilometres south on Highway 40 to the Picklejar Creek picnic area and trailhead on the east side of the road. Look for the horse loading ramp at the end of the loop parking lot; the trail begins immediately behind the ramp.

The hike: The Picklejar Creek trail has fallen into disuse over the years as hikers learned that it does not lead to Picklejar Lakes (see hike # 57–Picklejar Lakes). The first kilometre or two along the creek bottom is often flooded by seasonal runoff or beaver activity and the route is overgrown with alder, willow, and conifer saplings. Even where the tread can be discerned, it is difficult to follow through the tangle of foliage, and numerous side trails and game runs confuse the way. Take a compass and keep your hiking party within earshot of one another.

For some avid hikers, the challenge of following this trail is its main attraction. Few trails offers as much solitude so close to the road, and there is a high likelihood of seeing deer, elk, moose, or other wildlife. Song birds, raptors, and woodpeckers frequent the forest edge along the boggy, willow-clogged creek. Amateur botanists will delight in the variety of plant life, from moss-covered spruce trees to bog gentians and broadleaf strawberries. Finally, determined hikers are rewarded with a fine view of the upper Highwood River Valley, including Odlum Ridge, Mist Mountain, Storelk Mountain, and the peaks of the Highwood Range.

From the end of the parking lot at the Picklejar Creek picnic area, the trail dives into the dense wall of trees behind the horse loading ramp. Stay on the north bank of the creek, keeping to the higher ground whenever possible. The trail hugs the edge of the creek bottom for the first 600 metres and then contours gradually up the hillside on the left. About two kilometres in, the trees thin and the trail cuts left and uphill. Here the track grows even more indistinct; follow the dry, open valley one ridge removed from the north fork of Picklejar Creek.

The climb is hot after the jungle-like canopy over the lower trail, but soon a grassy saddle is reached between the shoulder of Mist Ridge and an outlying knob. Turn left to climb to the 2,400-metre top of the knob for a grand view of the divide range and Mist Mountain to the west and the Highwood Range to the northeast.

From the saddle, you can either retrace your steps down Picklejar Creek

HIKE 58 *PICKLEJAR CREEK*

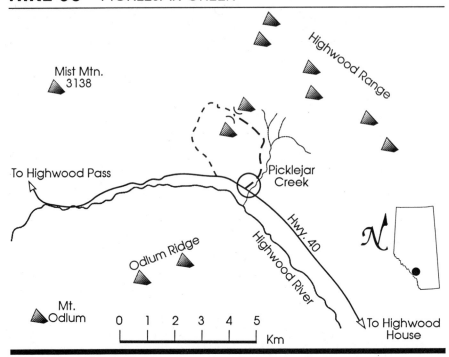

(and explore any one of the headwaters forks in the upper basin), or continue down the other side on an old road bed to the Mist Creek drainage. Turn left at each of the two ensuing junctions to reach the Mist Creek picnic area 500 metres north of the Picklejar Creek picnic area on Highway 40.

HIKE 59 *MIST CREEK*

General description: A moderate day hike to a series of alpine basins on the flanks of Mist and Storm mountains.
General location: Southeast of Highwood Pass near the boundary of Peter Lougheed Provincial Park in Kananaskis Country.
Maps: 82 J/10.
Special attractions: Alpine scenery, natural hot springs, off-trail hiking, wildlife.
For more information: Kananaskis Country, Suite 412, 1011 Glenmore Trail S.W., Calgary, Alberta, T2V 4R6. Ph: (403) 297-3362.
Finding the trailhead: From Highwood Pass, drive south eleven kilometres on Highway 40 to the Mist Creek picnic area and trailhead on the west side

of the road. The trail begins at the north end of the parking lot and immediately crosses the highway.

The hike: Mist Creek is sometimes used as a connecting route to the Sheep Creek trail, which links the Tombstone backcountry campground to Bluerock campground and the Junction Creek trailhead at the western terminus of Highway 546. Much of this route traverses old mining roads and packers' trails and is better suited to horse travel than backpacking. But for those willing to wander off trail and invest a modicum of energy to gain the upper slopes, a day's worth of exploration awaits on the northeast flank of Mist and Storm mountains.

After crossing Highway 40 follow the old mining road on the east side of Mist Creek for a little over one kilometre. Turn left onto the Mist Creek trail and continue the gradual climb along the banks of Mist Creek. The valley bottom is heavily timbered, but frequent bogs and meadows offer glimpses of the Mist Mountain escarpment to the west.

The first of four alpine basins comes into view below the summit ramparts about five kilometres from the trailhead. Ford the creek and climb the southern side of the bowl. By contouring in toward the stream and crossing to the north side of the drainage at timberline, strong hikers can ascend nearly to the 3,138-metre summit of Mist Mountain. Also keep an eye out for the small hot springs just above tree line, a feature that is easier to find on a cold autumn morning when steam rises in the crisp air.

HIKE 59 *MIST CREEK*

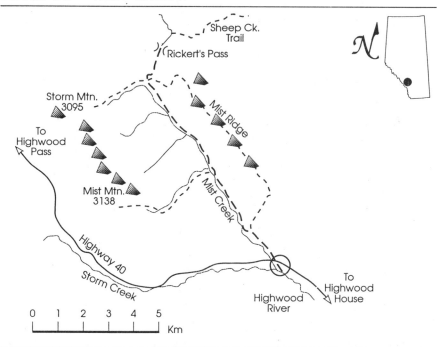

Three more basins lie to the north along the ridge between Mist Mountain and Storm Mountain. A full day can be spent wandering the upper reaches of any one of these bowls, and it's easy to loose track of time when preoccupied with the scenery and route-finding. Be sure to reserve enough daylight for the hike out.

The second basin ends against the sheer, almost overhanging, upper face of Mist Mountain, and the third and fourth bowls offer views of Rickert's Pass at the head of Mist Creek. By scrambling over steep talus and testing one's route-finding skills, it is possible to follow a high line between basins, but walking across the slope is hard on feet and boots, and much of the rock is loose or crumbly. Snowfields linger through July in some years and the snow may turn rotten in midday heat.

Less experienced hikers with a full day should consider staying on the main trail until it begins the climb to Rickert's Pass, about ten kilometres from the trailhead. From here, the fourth basin curves west to the banded wall of Storm Mountain. Stay low in the meadows along the tributary stream and scan the slopes above for elk, bighorn sheep, and mountain goat. Also watch for signs of the occasional grizzly bear.

Hikers wishing to stay on the trail can climb to Rickert's Pass, though the view down Sheep Creek is anticlimactic after hiking beneath Mist Mountain much of the way. Allow five or six hours for the twenty-kilometre roundtrip to the pass.

HIKE 60   *MOUNT ASSINIBOINE*

General description: A strenuous three- to five-day trek over two alpine passes to a large backcountry lake fed by icefields on the north face of Mount Assiniboine.

General location: The southern tip of Banff National Park along Alberta's western border, and the eastern section of Mount Assiniboine Provincial Park in British Columbia.

Maps: Banff National park; Mount Assiniboine Provincial Park; 82 J/13.

Special attractions: Outstanding alpine scenery, two high passes, innumerable lakes, wildlife, fishing.

For more information: Park Superintendent, Banff National Park, P.O. Box 900, Banff, Alberta, TOL OCO. Ph: (403) 762-3324. Or: Ministry of Parks, District Manager, Box 118, Wasa, British Columbia, VOB 2KO. Ph: (604) 422-3212.

Finding the trailhead: From the Smith-Dorrien/Spray Road south of Canmore, turn west onto the Mount Shark/Mount Engadine Lodge access road. Drive five kilometres to the parking lot and Mount Shark trailhead at the end of the road. The trail continues on the gated logging road from the western end of the lot.

The hike: At 3,618 metres, Mount Assiniboine is the highest peak in Banff National Park. Because it rises on the Continental Divide, the peak is also the

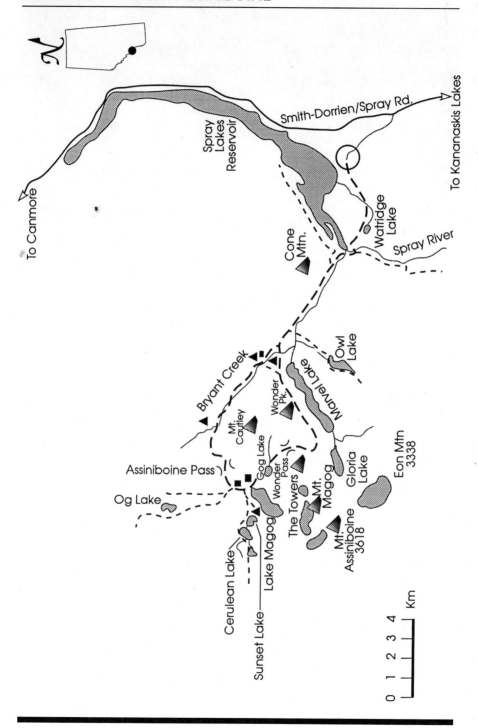

Mt. Assiniboine, the tallest mountain in Banff National Park. Randy Roch photo

tallest point in British Columbia's Mount Assiniboine Provincial Park. The mountain is an impressive sight from either side of the divide, a pyramid of rock and ice known as the "Matterhorn of the Rockies" for its resemblance to the famous landmark of the Swiss Alps.

But Mount Assiniboine is only one of many reasons hikers flock to this corner of the divide range. Here too are found shimmering lakes, massive glaciers, alpine meadows dappled with wildflowers, and large numbers of elk, deer, moose, bighorn sheep, and mountain goats. Black bears and grizzlies roam the forests, and wolverine and wolf leave traces of their passing. Despite growing popularity, a sense of wilderness and solitude prevails over much of this area.

The Mount Shark trailhead at the southwest end of Spray Lakes Reservoir offers perhaps the most scenic approach to Mount Assiniboine and the Magog Lake basin (see Hike # 61–Marvel Lake). From the trailhead, follow the old logging road past Watridge Lake to the boundary of Banff National Park. The logging road continues down to a bridge across the Spray River gorge, the inlet to Spray Lakes Reservoir. Turn right at the junction immediately beyond the bridge and walk 500 metres to another bridge and trail junction. Bear left here and follow the Bryant Creek trail northwest for six kilometres to the shortcut trail to Marvel Lake on the left. Leave the logging road and cross Bryant Creek as the trail contours past a small campground and on to Marvel Lake's eastern shore. Here the trail climbs gradually up the flank of Wonder Peak, traversing rock-strewn avalanche chutes and scattered stands of trees. At the junction with the Marvel Pass Trail above the lake's western end, turn right to begin the steep switchbacks to Wonder Pass.

The 2,377-metre pass is a narrow, barren gap between the cliffs of Wonder

Peak to the east and The Towers rising to 2,846 metres on the west. The view south toward Mount Eon and Marvel Peak is stunning, rivalled only by the expanse of the Magog and Og valleys to the north. From the pass the trail descends gently through meadows and subalpine timber, past Gog Lake, to the major trail junction and administrative centre below Lake Magog. Continue around the outlet of the lake and along the west shore to the Lake Magog Campground, twenty-five kilometres from the trailhead.

Plan to spend two nights at Lake Magog to allow for at least one full day of exploring the Sunburst Valley to the west. In inclement weather, many hikers opt to stay at the Naiset cabins near Park Headquarters and across Magog Creek from Assiniboine Lodge. There are four cabins with a total capacity of 29, and as of 1991 the fee was $6 per person each night. Bunk space is available on a first-come, first-served basis, and you'll need your own sleeping bag. The cabins usually fill up early, so don't neglect to pack a tent.

To complete the loop back to the Mount Shark trailhead, follow the Assiniboine Pass trail north from the Lake Magog Campground, past the Gog Lake/Sunburst Valley intersection 1.5 kilometres to the Nub Peak trail junction. Bear right, past Assiniboine Lodge, and begin the undulating climb to Assiniboine Pass. Keep to the right where the Og Pass trail (and horse route to Assiniboine Pass) branches left. The summit of the pass is reached in four kilometres of easy walking and though heavily timbered, it offers a fine view of Mount Assiniboine to the south.

The trail switchbacks down the Alberta side of the pass and forks just one kilometre from the summit. Follow the hiker's trail to the left to avoid the steep, rough horse path on the right. Over the next five kilometres the trail works its way down to Bryant Creek and continues another three kilometres to join the Allenby Trail. Turn right to cross Bryant Creek again and rejoin the old Bryant Creek logging road. A short path to the west leads to a designated campground, a good interim site to overnight on the long push out to the trailhead.

From here the road descends three kilometres along Bryant Creek to the warden's cabin and campground at the Marvel Lake trail junction. Retrace the route to Spray Lakes Reservoir and Watridge Lake to reach the Mount Shark trailhead. —*Randy Roch*

HIKE 61 *MARVEL LAKE*

General description: A long but moderate day hike or an easy overnighter to a large subalpine lake ringed by snow-covered peaks.
General location: The southern tip of Banff National Park, west of Spray Lakes Reservoir in Kananaskis Country.
Maps: Banff National Park; 82 J/13.
Special attractions: Watridge, Marvel, and Gloria lakes; Karst Spring; spectacular alpine views of Mount Assiniboine and surrounding peaks, renowned trout fishing.

For more information: Park Superintendent, Banff National Park, P.O. Box 900, Banff, Alberta, TOL OCO. Ph: (403) 762-3324. Or: Kananaskis Country, Suite 412, 1011 Glenmore Trail S.W., Calgary, Alberta, T2V 4R6. Ph: (403) 297-3362.

Finding the trailhead: From the Smith-Dorrien/Spray Road south of Canmore, turn west onto the Mount Shark/Mount Engadine Lodge access road. Drive five kilometres to the parking lot and Mount Shark trailhead at the end of the road. The trail continues on the gated logging road from the western end of the lot.

The hike: Marvel Lake is on the way to Wonder Pass, one of the more popular access routes to the Lake Magog basin in Mount Assiniboine Provincial Park in British Columbia (see hike #60–Mount Assiniboine). But the trout fishing in Marvel Lake is so good—and the scenery so spectacular—that this long, glacial-trough tarn has become a destination in its own right, one that will reward even the non-fishing day hiker.

From the trailhead, follow the old logging road a little over three kilometres to Watridge Lake, a beautiful forested pool nudging the boundary of Banff National Park. Follow the trail to the left 100 metres to reach the lake's eastern shore. There is excellent cutthroat trout fishing here, a splendid view of Cone Mountain to the north, and a side trail south leads to Karst Spring, a massive upwelling of fresh water from the north flank of Mount Shark.

From the Watridge Lake junction, continue along the logging road into Banff National Park and down to the stout bridge across the Spray River gorge, the inlet to Spray Lakes Reservoir. Turn right at the junction immediately beyond the bridge and walk 500 metres to another bridge and trail junction. Bear left here and follow the Bryant Creek trail northwest along the foot of Cone Mountain.

Five kilometres from the Bryant Creek bridge, the route to Owl Lake branches to the left. Proceed straight ahead, climbing steadily for another kilometre to the short-cut trail to Marvel Lake on the left. Leave the logging road and cross Bryant Creek as the trail contours past a small campground and on to Marvel Lake's eastern end, 1.5 kilometres from the Bryant Creek trail.

The trough that holds Marvel Lake was carved by a massive glacier that once spilled from the western face of 3,618-metre Mount Assiniboine, the "Matterhorn" shaped peak rising above the far end of the lake. Glaciers still cling to Assiniboine and surrounding crags, but the trough now holds Gloria and Marvel lakes, the latter of which is famed for cutthroat trout. It is not uncommon to see fly-fishermen struggling to land fish too big for their nets.

A crude anglers' trail follows the lakeshore, but the official trail swings high on the slopes above the lake, crossing scoured avalanche chutes and passing through open bands of trees. About 4.5 kilometres from the east end of Marvel Lake, the trail forks right and uphill to Wonder Pass and left (down) to the west end of Marvel Lake. Strong day hikers can drop to Marvel Creek just above the inlet and turn right to reach Gloria Lake, a smaller tarn near the head of an impressive cirque.

Though this area receives heavy use during the peak of the hiking season, wildlife is still abundant. Watch for elk, deer, moose, coyotes, and bears—

both black and grizzly. Wolves are less frequently seen, but campers may hear them at dawn or dusk.

Attempting Marvel Lake as a day hike requires some forethought. Total roundtrip distance to the lake's east end is twenty-nine kilometres, though much of this is over gently graded trail with little elevation gain. Many people ride mountain bikes along the old logging road up Bryant Creek, saving several hours of walking. If you want more time for fishing or exploring the upper basin, pack for an overnight and stay at the small campground one kilometre below Marvel Lake.

Whichever approach you use, go prepared for weather. Marvel Lake lies

HIKE 61   *MARVEL LAKE*

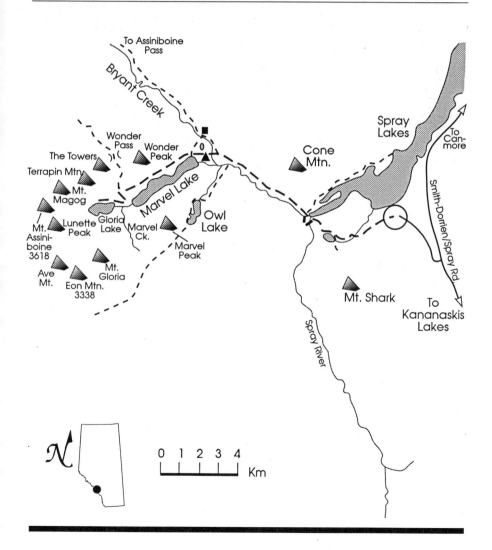

Watch for elk on the way to Marvel Lake.

near the base of a series of 3,000-metre peaks that generate their own precipitation and winds. Carry rain gear, an extra layer of insulating clothes, and plenty of food. Realize that storms can arrive quickly here and temperatures may plummet without warning. If the weather turns for the worst, head for the trail shelter one kilometre south of the Bryant Creek warden's cabin on the Bryant Creek trail. —*Randy Roch*

HIKE 62 *GALATEA LAKES*

General description: An easy day hike or overnight along Galatea Creek to a pair of high cirque lakes below the east face of Mount Engadine.

General location: South of Nakiska ski area on the west side of Highway 40 in Kananaskis Country.

Maps: Ribbon/Spray Summer Trails brochure; 82 J/14.

Special attractions: Lillian and Galatea lakes, views of Mount Engadine, good opportunities for backcountry day hiking, fishing, abundant wildlife.

For more information: Kananaskis Country, Suite 412, 1011 Glenmore Trail S.W., Calgary, Alberta, T2V 4R6. Ph: (403) 297-3362.

Finding the trailhead: Drive south on Highway 40 to the Galatea picnic area and trailhead on the west side of the road about eighteen kilometres south of the Nakiska ski area access road. The trail begins on an old road at the west end of the lot, crossing the Kananaskis River on a stout suspension bridge.

The hike: The trek up Galatea Creek to Lillian Lake and the two Galatea Lakes is popular with good reason. The trail follows a lush riparian corridor rich in brilliant wildflowers and replete with wildlife, eventually arriving at a forested lake and cozy campground that serves as a good base camp for day

HIKE 62 *GALATEA LAKES*

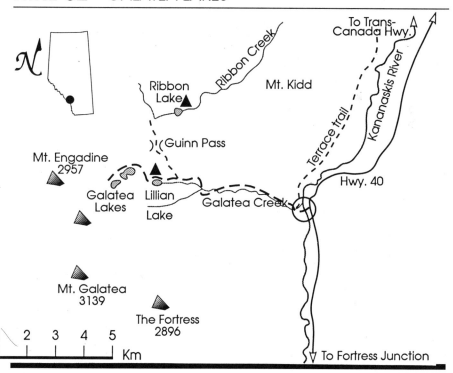

hikes to the Galatea cirque or to the summit of Guinn Pass. Strong hikers can walk the eight kilometres to Upper Galatea Lake and return to the trailhead in a day, but the area warrants an overnight.

After crossing the suspension bridge over the Kananaskis River, the trail crosses Galatea Creek and joins the Terrace trail running south from the Ribbon Creek trailhead at Nakiska. Turn left here and climb into the Galatea Valley, crossing the creek several times on good log bridges.

The route continues along the creek through dense timber and shoulder-high cow parsnip. Just below the forks of Galatea Creek, the trail crosses to the north bank again and begins a steady climb along the north fork. The trail to Guinn Pass branches uphill to the right 5.5 kilometres from the trailhead. Another kilometre straight ahead brings you to the east shore of Lillian Lake.

Lillian is popular with day hikers for its fishing, picnicking, and even swimming on hot days. The campground here is large by backcountry standards but can fill up on busy weekends. The trail runs along the north shore of the lake to the campground at the west end.

To reach Galatea Lakes, follow the rough track leading uphill from campsite 11. The trail traverses a talus slope at the top of this gentle headwall and then dips down to the first lake. Follow the scant trail around the north shore and over a low ridge to the second lake set beneath a sheer wall at the foot of Mount Engadine.

As a side trip for campers staying at Lillian Lake, the grunt up Guinn Pass offers excellent views of Mount Galatea and The Fortress to the south, and a fair chance of seeing deer, elk, bighorn sheep, or possibly a bear on the open slopes below the summit. The pass lies about 1.5 kilometres above the junction with the Galatea Creek trail, and roughly 450 metres higher in elevation. This steep, hot climb is best done early in the morning or as an evening stroll. If you have a full day to explore, consider continuing over the pass to Ribbon Lake, 5.5 kilometres from Lillian Lake.

HIKE 63 *WASOOTCH CREEK*

General description: An easy day hike along the gravel outwash flats of Wasootch Creek.

General location: Six kilometres northwest of the Nakiska ski area on the east side of Highway 40 in Kananaskis Country.

Maps: Ribbon/Spray Summer Trails brochure; 82 J/14.

Special attractions: Rock climbing, the Wasootch Tower, good opportunities for solitude.

For more information: Kananaskis Country, Suite 412, 1011 Glenmore Trail S.W., Calgary, Alberta, T2V 4R6. Ph: (403) 297-3362.

Finding the trailhead: Turn east onto the Wasootch Creek access road six kilometres north of Nakiska ski area on Highway 40. The road winds for 500 metres to a parking lot on the gravel flats of Wasootch Creek. A well-worn trail leaves from the south corner of the lot onto the gravel flats.

The hike: Most visitors to Wasootch Creek come to hone rock climbing skills on the Wasootch Slabs, a series of smooth rock faces on the east bank of the creek bed. A one-kilometre trail provides easy access to these slabs for climbers and spectators alike. Few people travel beyond the end of this track, however, and the valley beyond offers a sense of solitude rarely found so near the road.

The gravel flats here allow easy walking, though sturdy boots will help protect your ankles from scrapes and unexpected twists. The first kilometre favours the east side of the creek bottom near the foot of the practice slabs. The white letters on the rocks were painted there by the Canadian army,

HIKE 63 *WASOOTCH CREEK*

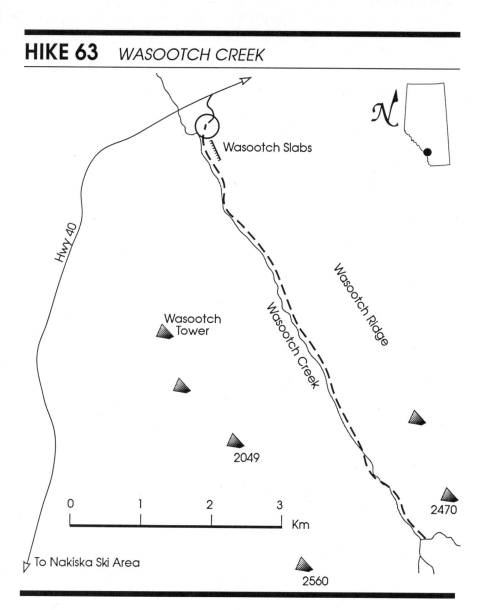

which used the slabs to train soldiers for mountaineering. On the west side of the valley, the Wasootch Tower thrusts skyward with an unusual corkscrew effect.

From the end of the established trail, it is possible to walk another five kilometres along the dry creek bottom unimpeded by forest or slope. Chickadees and woodpeckers flit across the drainage from one forested slope to the other, and occasionally the stream breaks out of its stony bed to run above ground before vanishing again. But silence reigns here, and one can readily imagine the canyon as it was in prehistoric times, domain of the indians who came here for stones for their mortars and pestles, axe heads, and arrowheads.

Six kilometres from the trailhead the trees close in on the creek bottom and the stream forks right and left. Find a shady spot for lunch and a nap. Return by the same route.

HIKE 64 *NIHAHI RIDGE*

General description: A short but strenuous day hike to a windswept ridge top overlooking the Little Elbow Valley.

General location: At the terminus of Highway 66 west of Bragg Creek in Kananaskis Country.

Maps: 82 J/15.

Special attractions: Excellent views of the Little Elbow River Valley and Mounts Remus and Romulus, the distant Opal Range, wildflowers, some wildlife.

For more information: Kananaskis Country, Suite 412, 1011 Glenmore Trail S.W., Calgary, Alberta, T2V 4R6. Ph: (403) 297-3362.

Finding the trailhead: Drive west twenty-six kilometres from Bragg Creek on Highway 66 to the end of the road at the Little Elbow Campground. Day-use visitors should park in the small lot on the righthand side of the road across from the hikers' bridge over the Little Elbow River. The Little Elbow Interpretive Trail begins by the bridge's on-ramp, keeping to the north bank of the river. Follow this path for one kilometre to the gate on the Little Elbow road at campground loop E. Continue past the gate and down the road for one kilometre to a single-track footpath leading into the trees on the right. Look for the trail sign.

The hike: Nihahi Ridge is the perfect destination for day hikers looking for some exercise, good views, and a chance to acquaint themselves with the lay of the land in the Little Elbow region of Kananaskis Country. The trip is short—only five kilometres to the best vantage point atop the ridge—but scenic over most of its length. The steep sections are humbling, but scrambling up the scree and rock benches can be fun if the pace is relaxed and the weather cooperates.

Travel light, but do carry plenty of drinking water and a good windbreaker. If you want to gain the best views, wear sturdy shoes suitable for a

Nihahi Ridge offers views deep into the Little Elbow River country.

little non-technical rock climbing.

After walking the Little Elbow Interpretive Trail and the kilometre of road, take the first footpath to the right. This trail winds through the forest for 200 metres then joins the Little Elbow horse path. Turn left and walk another 100 metres to a second junction: the horse path continues straight ahead and the Nihahi Ridge Trail breaks uphill to the right.

The trail climbs immediately, snaking its way through a shrubby forest to the top of a low rise which gives the first glimpse of the scenery to come. Wildflowers are abundant here in the spring, and deer and elk are sometimes seen on the slopes to the west. The trail contours along this windy ridge to cross the top of a small open bowl at the southern end of Nihahi Ridge. Back in the trees, the trail angles upward to the bare spine of the ridge, and hikers must scramble up the last fifteen metres with the aid of a handrail.

From here the trail climbs in fits and starts, keeping to the crest of the ridge or just to the leeward side. About midway up the ridge a grassy saddle is reached, marked with a cairn, offering a fair view of the mountains in the foreground. Many casual hikers consider this a good turnaround point, but the ridgeline beckons with promises of a higher perch.

From the saddle, climb the short staircase of boulders to gain the next crest of the ridge and follow the trail as it dips along the leeward side, then more directly on the ridgeline. Shortly after clambering onto a particularly rocky patch on the crest, the trail cuts back to the lee side again and braids into a number of "goat trails" toward the top. The slope is steep and covered with loose, plate-like scree that threatens to slide at every step. Pick your footing carefully and be especially wary of stones loosened by hikers above.

The scree slope eventually ends where the forest rises to meet the solid

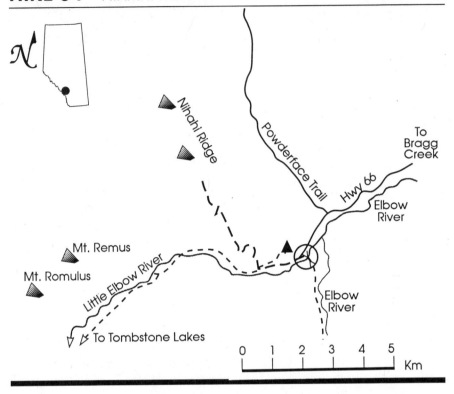

hogback of rock that caps the ridge. A single dirt trail emerges from the numerous routes on the scree and threads between the trees and the hogback with no view to either side. Several short chimneys in the hogback offer access to the ridge top if you're prepared to climb hand and foot for ten metres or so. Climb carefully and stay within the limits of your experience and skill.

A blast of wind will likely greet you on top, and with it the outstanding vista as the uninterrupted slab of Nihahi Ridge falls away to the Little Elbow River winding between Mount Remus and Mount Romulus on the right and Mount Glasgow and Mount Cornwall on the left. The Opal Range runs above the headwaters in the distance. Many people are so taken with this view that they neglect to glance east to the foothills and plains. Look to this horizon and you'll see the silvery skyline of Calgary some sixty-five kilometres distant.

Retrace your steps, being particularly cautious on the climb down from the hogback and on the steep pitches of scree. Watch for hikers coming up and try to avoid releasing stones as you descend. Total roundtrip distance is ten kilometres.

HIKE 65   *ELBOW LOOP*

General description: A moderate three to five day backpack on old roads and wide trails through the Front Range of the Canadian Rockies.

General location: West of the western terminus of Highway 66 in Kananaskis Country.

Maps: 82 J/10, 82 J/15.

Special attractions: Outstanding mountain scenery, Tombstone Lakes, wildlife, fishing.

For more information: Kananaskis Country, Suite 412, 1011 Glenmore Trail S.W., Calgary, Alberta, T2V 4R6. Ph: (403) 297-3362.

Finding the trailhead: Drive west twenty-six kilometres from Bragg Creek on Highway 66 to the end of the road at the Little Elbow campground. Park in the equestrian lot just beyond the end of the pavement. Walk down the campground access road to the Little Elbow interpretive trail, which begins at the foot of a suspension bridge across the Little Elbow River. Keep to the north bank of the river and follow this path for one kilometre to the gate on the Little Elbow road at campground loop E. Continue past the gate and down the road to begin the hike.

The hike: The Big and Little Elbow trails form a thirty-eight- kilometre loop of comparatively easy hiking through the valleys and peaks of the Front Range west of Calgary. Though the scenery is spectacular, most of the route follows old roads, and a heavily-used horse trail weaves on and off the main track for the entire loop. In recent years, even bicyclists have swarmed the trail in increasing numbers, so hikers should look elsewhere for the serenity of a wilderness experience.

Nevertheless, the Elbow Loop is an enjoyable trek, offering unlimited opportunities for off-the-beaten-path forays and side trips on adjoining trails. And Little Elbow Pass—near the mid-point of the hike—is a small slice of backcountry heaven, fringed in delicate larches and well worth the sometimes tedious walk in.

From the gate by the Little Elbow campground, walk down the old road on the north bank of the Little Elbow River. One kilometre from the gate, the Nihahi Ridge trail cuts uphill to the right, and another 2.5 kilometres of hiking brings you to the Nihahi Creek trail, also branching right. Continue straight ahead 500 metres to an old bridge painted blue, which crosses to the south bank. From here, the hiker's trail remains on the south bank for nearly eight kilometres to the Mount Romulus campground. About 800 metres from the blue bridge, the horse path forks to the right—this route is best avoided by hikers because it fords the Little Elbow River four times on the way to Mount Romulus.

From the Mount Romulus campground, the road bends south beside the Little Elbow River. This leg of the loop—seven kilometres of dreary, dusty road—is the poorest section of the trail and is best endured with a good conversation or a song in one's head. The reward is a wonderful, single-track trail that leaves the road just after the second crossing of the stream. Turn

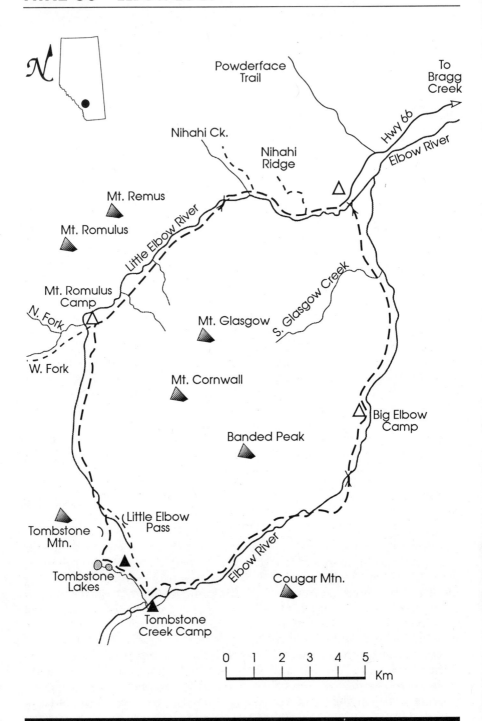

Powderface
Trail

To
Bragg
Creek

Nihahi Ck.

Nihahi
Ridge

Hwy 66

Elbow River

Mt. Remus

Little Elbow River

Mt. Romulus

Mt. Romulus
Camp

N. Fork

S. Glasgow Creek

Mt. Glasgow

W. Fork

Mt. Cornwall

Big Elbow
Camp

Banded Peak

Tombstone
Mtn.

Little Elbow
Pass

Tombstone
Lakes

Elbow River

Cougar Mtn.

Tombstone
Creek Camp

0 1 2 3 4 5

Km

right on a narrow jeep trail and walk past the weather station. The trail dwindles to a foot path that climbs steadily into a sun-dappled forest of larches beneath Tombstone Mountain. This broad pass tops out at 2,286 metres, and then the trail descends quickly into thick timber and the horsepackers' camp at Lower Tombstone Lake.

Turn left from the camp and follow Tombstone Creek down to the road again, which shortly joins the Big Elbow trail. Turn right and walk 600 metres to the Tombstone Creek campground, on the south side of the road immediately after crossing the creek.

To complete the loop, walk back to the intersection with the Little Elbow Road and bear right. The Big Elbow Road rolls high above the Elbow River in and out of meadows on the north flank of the valley for 2.5 kilometres before dropping down to the stream and joining with the horse trail. Five hundred metres further, the hiking trail forks right, running beside the river for another two kilometres only to rejoin the horse route again.

From here the trail undulates along the north bank of the river at the foot of Banded Mountain, descending into a narrow, shadowy canyon. Bear right after crossing the river and return to the road two kilometres downstream after a second bridge. Continue downstream to the Big Elbow campground beside the hiker trail on the right. The day's distance from Tombstone Creek campground to Big Elbow is twelve kilometres.

The final seven-kilometre leg follows the old road out, keeping to the west side of the river all the way to the bridge over the Little Elbow River and trail's end. The way is flat and uninspiring, but lasts only an hour or so. A cold soak for the feet in the Little Elbow River completes the trip.

Peter Lougheed Provincial Park

Peter Lougheed Provincial Park is the 509-square-kilometre neighbor to the west of Kananaskis Country. The park is studded with lakes and rippled with glacier-carved mountains, and a well-maintained web of hiking trails reaches into nearly every corner of this rugged wilderness.

Trails run the gamut from hundred-metre interpretive walks to week-long treks through remote alpine backcountry. The park even maintains paved trails for bicycle and wheelchair use, and the William Watson Lodge offers barrier-free accommodations for people who use wheelchairs or have limited mobility. And some of the best hiking is found off trail, on the flanks of barren mountains or through trackless valley forests.

Weather here can change in a wink, from sunny and clear to snow or blustery sleet and rain. Heavy snowpack lingers through July and winter storms may strike as early as September. Temperatures can dip below freezing any season of the year, particularly at night in the higher elevations.

Wildlife is plentiful, and some trails are prone to closure due to bear activity. Always check with a warden or park staff member before heading into the backcountry to obtain up-to-date trail information. To obtain the summer trails brochure and other materials, write to the Park Superintendent, Peter Lougheed Provincial Park, Box 130, Kananaskis Village, Alberta, T0L 2H0.

HIKE 66 *PTARMIGAN CIRQUE*

General description: An easy two- to three-hour walk through the harsh mountain environment above timberline.
General location: Atop Highwood Pass on Highway 40 near the southern border of Peter Lougheed Provincial Park.
Maps: Peter Lougheed Provincial Park Summer Trails brochure; 82 J/10.
Special attractions: Interpretive trail with brochure, spectacular alpine scenery, wildflowers, some wildlife.

HIKE 66 *PTARMIGAN CIRQUE*

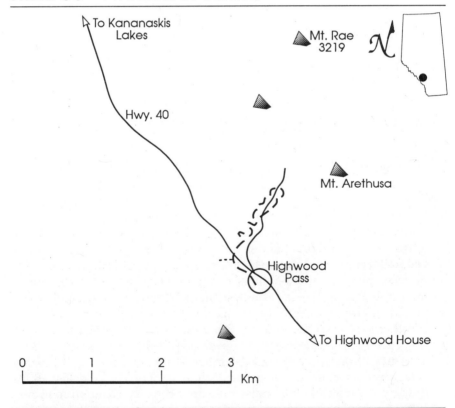

For more information: Park Superintendent, Peter Lougheed Provincial Park, Box 130, Kananaskis Village, Alberta, TOL 2HO. Ph: (403) 591-7222.

Finding the trailhead: From the junction of Highway 40 and the Kananaskis Lakes Trail, drive fifteen kilometres south on Highway 40 to the summit of Highwood Pass. Park in the large lot on the west side of the road about 200 metres south of the summit. The trail begins at the north end of the parking lot behind the trail sign and brochure dispenser.

The hike: Ptarmigan Cirque is a small, glacier-carved notch between Mount Rae and Mount Arethusa on the western flank of the Misty Range. This lofty basin hangs directly above Highway 40, allowing relatively easy access to an alpine world of boulder fields, brilliant wildflowers, and bighorn sheep.

Most hikers can comfortably walk the seven-kilometre-loop trail into Ptarmigan Cirque in two hours or less, but even for this short a time a jacket and a warm hat will come in handy. Also carry drinking water and binoculars, and don't neglect to pick up the interpretive brochure at the trailhead.

The trail shares the first kilometre with a much shorter interpretive hike through Highwood Meadows, the broad shrubby summit of Highwood Pass. Turn right on the gravel path where the Highwood Meadows boardwalk begins and cross to the east side of Highway 40. From here the trail climbs quickly though shady stands of subalpine fir and spruce, also crossing several open slopes studded with glacier lilies, Indian paintbrush, aster, and arrowleaf balsamroot.

The trail forks about 1.5 kilometres after crossing the road. Take the left fork to follow the sequence of stops in the interpretive brochure. The trail

Just three kilometres above the highway, Ptarmigan Cirque is the most accessible alpine basin in Peter Lougheed Provincial Park.

soon emerges above timberline and levels off as it leads into the cirque. Many of the broken rocks and boulders beside the trail contain fossils of ancient coral; also watch here for white-tailed ptarmigan, motionless and well-camouflaged among the rocks.

Leaving the flank of Mount Rae, the trail crosses a small stream and begins the leg back to the highway. Those tempted to wander into the upper basin should tread lightly and try to keep off the fragile soil by rock-hopping whenever possible. The loop back to the main trail is direct and gently graded. A short spur trail just above timberline leads to a viewpoint over a small waterfall. This is also a good spot for glassing the mountainsides for bighorn sheep or the occasional grizzly bear.

HIKE 67   *MOUNT INDEFATIGABLE*

General description: A strenuous half-day hike with spectacular views of the Kananaskis Lakes and surrounding mountains.
General location: West shore of Lower Kananaskis Lake, in Peter Lougheed Provincial Park.
Maps: Peter Lougheed Provincial Park trails map; 82 J/11.
Special attractions: Open views of Upper and Lower Kananaskis Lakes over most of the trail; option to climb to the summit of Mount Indefatigable.
For more information: Park Superintendent, Peter Lougheed Provincial Park, Box 130, Kananaskis Village, Alberta, TOL 2HO. Ph: (403) 591-7222.

Lower Kananaskis Lake from Mount Indefatigable.

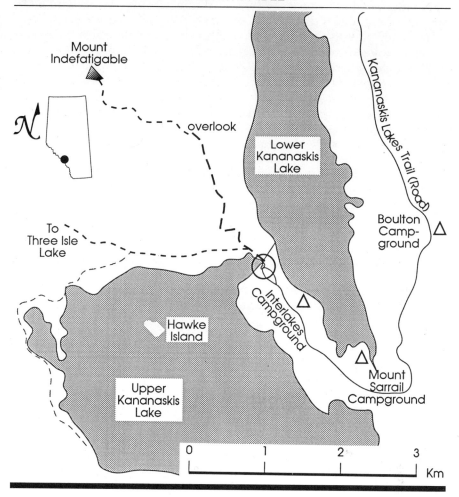

Finding the trailhead: Turn west onto the Kananaskis Lakes Trail from Kananaskis Trail (Highway 40). Follow this road to its terminus at the North Interlakes parking lot next to the earthen dam. Walk across the dam and spillway and turn left onto the old fire road. Roughly seventy metres from the spillway, turn onto the footpath that cuts uphill to the right.

The hike: Few trails in the Canadian Rockies offer views as stunning as the panorama that unfolds from this four-kilometre trail. Upper and Lower Kananaskis Lakes sparkle at the base of Mount Indefatigable, and the ramparts of the Opal, Misty, and Elk mountain ranges rise to the east, stretching as far as the eye can see from north to south.

At first, the trail wends through a dense forest of mixed conifers, crosses a small creek, and then switchbacks quickly to the runout of a narrow avalanche gully. The original trail stays on the western side of the gully and offers no views initially. A more recent trail climbs immediately onto an open ridge of crumbly rock and thin soil. From here the climb is hard work, stair-stepping quickly up the ridge and open to the full bore of the sun. You'll want to stop often as each new increment of elevation gained brings more of the lakes and surrounding mountains into view.

A wooden bench welcomes hikers to the first level resting spot and overlook. Another good vantage point lies just another 100 metres above the bench, and the final overlook, providing unobstructed views north and east, is reached on the spur on the flank of Mount Indefatigable's southern summit.

If this steep ascent hasn't drained your legs and lungs, you may wish to continue on to the actual summit at 2,651 metres, capped by a radio tower. There is no trail, but the most straightforward route climbs directly up the avalanche slopes of the southern summit, then crosses near the top onto the conspicuous saddle. From here, the main summit to the north is an easy scramble. Be sure to carry plenty of water, a camera, and a pair of binoculars.

HIKE 68   *THREE ISLE LAKE*

General description: An easy overnight or moderate day hike to a large subalpine lake tucked below the Continental Divide.
General location: West of Kananaskis Lakes in Peter Lougheed Provincial Park.
Maps: Peter Lougheed Provincial Park Summer Trails brochure; 82 J/11.
Special attractions: Upper Kananaskis Lake, Three Isle Lake, outstanding mountain scenery, wildlife.
For more information: Park superintendent, Peter Lougheed Provincial Park, Box 130, Kananaskis Village, Alberta, TOL 2HO. Ph: (403) 591-7222.
Finding the trailhead: Turn west onto the Kananaskis Lakes Trail from Kananaskis Trail (Highway 40). Follow this road to its terminus at the North Interlakes parking lot next to the earthen dam. Walk across the dam and spillway and turn left onto the old fire road.

The hike: For scenery and ease of access to the backcountry, few trails match the route into Three Isle Lake near the western boundary of Peter Lougheed Provincial Park. Hikers enjoy excellent views of Upper Kananaskis Lake and surrounding mountains in the early going, and the trail runs nearly level for much of the first seven kilometres of this twelve-kilometre hike. The final destination, a large subalpine lake cupped below the bulk of Mount Worthington, offers a pleasant backcountry campground and unrivalled opportunities for day hiking above timberline.

The first six kilometres follow an old fire road that rolls through the forest above the north shore of Upper Kananaskis Lake. Two and one-half kilometres from the trailhead, the main track drops from a junction with the upper lakes trail and eventually crosses the Upper Kananaskis River on a stout log

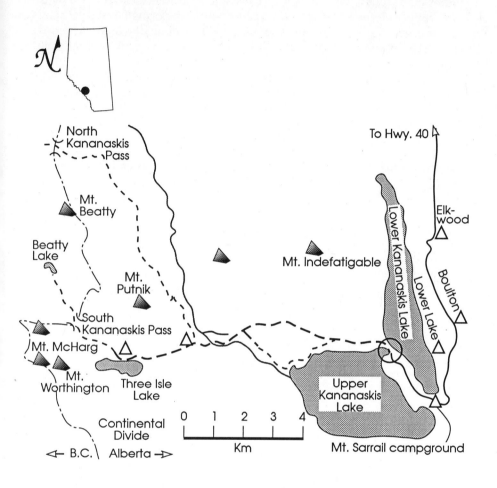

North
Kananaskis
Pass

To Hwy. 40

Mt.
Beatty

Elk-
wood

Beatty
Lake

Lower Kananaskis Lake

Mt. Indefatigable

Boulton

Mt.
Putnik

Lower Lake

South
Kananaskis Pass

Mt. McHarg

Mt.
Worthington   Three Isle
Lake

Upper
Kananaskis
Lake

Continental
Divide

0   1   2   3   4
Km

B.C. \ Alberta

Mt. Sarrail campground

bridge. Shortly after the bridge, the main track meets the Lyautey trail and then runs two kilometres to the Forks, where the Lawson trail branches to the right. A set of campsites straddles the Lawson trail just beyond the junction.

From Forks the trail climbs beside Three Isle Creek toward a steep headwall guarding the lake basin. After leaving the creek (which drains not from the lake but from the glaciers on Mount Northover to the south), the trail switchbacks up the face of the headwall, crossing from right to left before attaining the lip and dropping down to the lake's eastern shore. The Three Isle Campground lies on the northeast end of the lake, providing a good base camp from which to explore the basin.

The most popular day hike from camp consists of following the main trail along the north shore of Three Isle Lake and climbing to South Kananaskis Pass, two kilometres from the campground. The pass offers views down Beatty Creek into British Columbia and north along the divide. For even better vistas, climb west to a large cairn and continue another 1,500 metres over rolling alpine terrain to the unnamed summit north of Mount McHarg. To the north, Palliser Pass and the rugged peaks along the southern border of Banff National Park come into view, while west and south the deep valley of the Palliser River falls away.

Most hikers return to Upper Kananaskis Lake by retracing their steps, but if time allows, a more adventurous loop can be completed by descending Beatty Creek and traversing North Kananaskis Pass to Turbine Canyon (see hike # 69–Turbine Canyon Loop).

HIKE 69   *TURBINE CANYON LOOP*

General description: A moderate three-to-five day backpack for experienced mountaineers along the headwaters of the Kananaskis River in the high country of the Continental Divide.
General location: West of Kananaskis Lakes in Peter Lougheed Provincial Park.
Maps: Peter Lougheed Provincial Park Summer Trails brochure; 82 J/11.
Special attractions: Tremendous alpine scenery; views of Haig and Beatty glaciers; Turbine Canyon; Lawson, Maude, Beatty, and Three Isle lakes; fishing; wildlife.
For more information: Park superintendent, Peter Lougheed Provincial Park, Box 130, Kananaskis Village, Alberta, TOL 2HO. Ph: (403) 591-7222.
Finding the trailhead: Turn west onto the Kananaskis Lakes Trail from Kananaskis Trail (Highway 40). Follow this road to its terminus at the North Interlakes parking lot next to the earthen dam. Walk across the dam and spillway and turn left onto the old fire road.

The hike: The majority of campers at Three Isle Lake spend an evening or one day tramping the slopes above base camp before heading back to the trailhead on the same route they followed in. But more adventurous trekkers can cross South Kananaskis Pass into the Palliser Valley, regain the divide on North Kananaskis Pass, and thus complete a forty-two-kilometre loop through some of the most rugged terrain in Peter Lougheed Provincial Park.

From the outlet of Upper Kananaskis Lake, follow the Three Isle trail to the campground at Three Isle Lake (see hike # 68 —Three Isle Lake). If time allows, spend an additional day at Three Isle Lake, exploring the basin and resting for the second—and hardest—leg of the loop.

From Three Isle Lake, follow the trail two kilometres to South Kananaskis Pass on the Continental Divide. Descend into the upper meadows of the Beatty Creek drainage, bearing north on the trail as it skirts Beatty Lake. From here the trail crosses the outlet and bends west down a short, dry

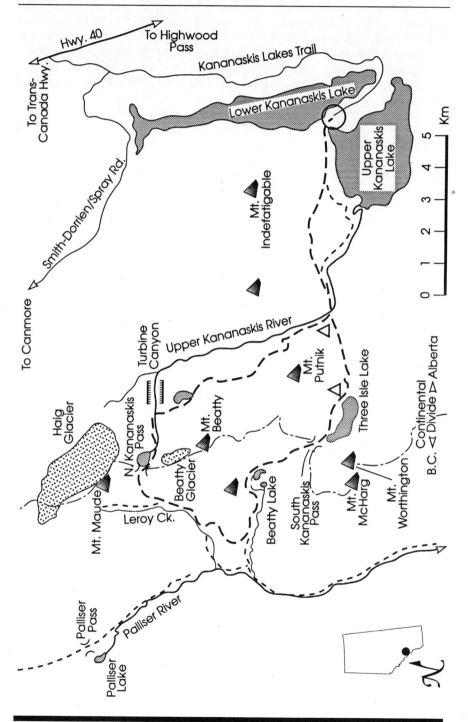

canyon—the stream runs underground. The canyon ends abruptly atop a precipitous headwall of loose scree, and the trail dives onto this slope, losing over 300 metres of elevation in one kilometre.

As the route begins a second breath-stopping pitch over an even steeper headwall, turn north and climb to the broad bench on the ridge running from the unnamed peak to the east. A vague trail traverses this outlier of Mount Beatty, rounding the corner and leading northeast above LeRoy Creek only to dwindle and vanish in a vast thicket of willows. Try to hold your elevation as you go, aiming for a wide avalanche chute that offers easier passage down to LeRoy Creek and the established trail along the creek bottom. While bushwhacking through this section, pay particular heed to bear signs and make plenty of noise.

Ford LeRoy Creek and join the trail running upstream. From the avalanche chute, it is about three kilometres to the summit of North Kananaskis Pass, bearing right at the trail junction at the forks of LeRoy Creek and climbing madly straight up the old outlet ravine from Maude Lake.

From the pass, cairns mark the trail as it banks to the south shore of Maude Lake, a windy, barren tarn. Beatty Glacier looms ahead, and the trail cuts below it to a low rise over the lake. Then the route drops down to Maude Brook and follows it into the trees to Turbine Canyon Campground, a little over two kilometres from the pass and some twelve kilometres from Three Isle Lake.

Again, an extra day at the campground provides time for rest and recreation. Anglers will want to backtrack to Maude Lake for excellent trout fishing, and everyone will be impressed by the deep, sinuous gorge of Turbine Canyon, a short side trip downstream from the campground.

The final leg of the loop is the easiest, though also the longest. Cross Maude Brook and pass the warden's cabin, and continue down trail to the west shore of Lawson Lake. The trail rolls along a broad shoulder on the east face of Mount Beatty and then drops 450 metres over the next 2.5 kilometres to the west bank of the Upper Kananaskis River. Within another kilometre you pass the Forks campground and rejoin the Three Isle Lake trail eight kilometres from the trailhead.

HIKE 70 *CHESTER LAKE*

General description: An easy day hike or overnight to a small subalpine lake in the Kananaskis Range.
General location: In the northern corner of Peter Lougheed Provincial Park, directly west of Fortress Mountain ski area.
Maps: Peter Lougheed Provincial Park Summer Trails brochure; 82 J/14.
Special attractions: Mountain scenery, wildlife, wildflowers, Chester Lake, fishing.
For more information: Park Superintendent, Peter Lougheed Provincial Park, Box 130, Kananaskis Village, Alberta, TOL 2HO. Ph: (403) 591-7222.
Finding the trailhead: From the Trans-Canada Highway, drive fifty

kilometres south on Highway 40 to the junction with the Kananaskis Lakes Trail. Turn right and drive 2.5 kilometres and turn right again onto the Smith-Dorrien/Spray Road heading north. Continue north for twenty-five kilometres to the Chester Lake trailhead and parking lot. The trail begins on the road berm at the north end of the lot behind the restrooms.

The hike: Like many trails in Peter Lougheed Provincial Park, the route to Chester Lake more than compensates for a dreary start by finishing at a sparkling tarn set amidst waves of wildflowers and craggy peaks. Anglers will find the added pleasure of hooking cutthroat trout out of the clear water,

HIKE 70   *CHESTER LAKE*

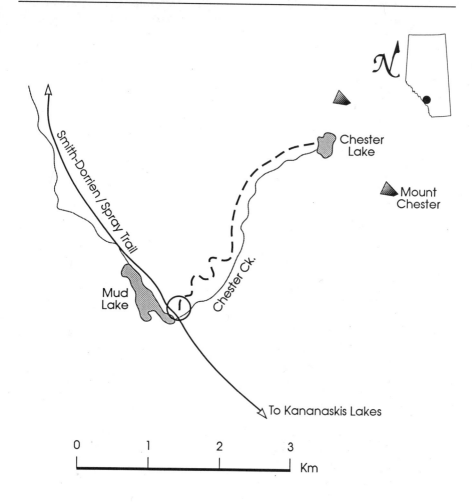

although fishing pressure at Chester Lake is so acute that park officials have set a catch limit of two fish per day.

The trail begins on a wide gravel road heading east from the parking lot. Pass the gate and turn left at the fork 100 metres ahead. The road immediately crosses Chester Creek and enters an old clearcut now choked with fireweed, alder, and slash. Stay on the road as it switchbacks uphill, climbing steadily and often looping directly above itself.

Two and one-half kilometres in, a foot path breaks uphill to the left just as the road begins to dip south toward the creek again. The trail climbs heartily for one kilometre through dense timber and levels off as it comes within earshot of the creek. From here the trail rolls 1.5 kilometres through brushy meadows and bands of fir above the gently meandering stream to the lake.

The flanks of Mount Chester tumble down to the water's edge to the southeast and the outlet stream points to the distant peaks of the northern Spray Range. The best campsites are found in the trees north and west of the lake, and anglers should obtain a fishing survey card from the box thirty

Mount Chester looms over Chester Lake.

metres from the west shore.

The high country around the lake is also worth exploring for those with good route-finding skills. A faint trail runs north through the larch and fir to a small pool at timberline. The feeder stream leads to two more pools cached in a canyon below Mount Galatea. Watch for mountain goats on the slopes above.

Another track climbs the low headwall on the northeast shore of Chester Lake. The cliff guards a narrow, rocky cirque—the true headwaters of Chester Creek—with its own tarn at the base of The Fortress. Either of these side treks requires about two hours roundtrip.

HIKE 71 *HEADWALL LAKES*

General description: A moderate day hike or overnight to a pair of alpine lakes nestled in a spectacular cirque below Mount Chester and The Fortress.
General location: In the northern corner of Peter Lougheed Provincial Park, on the west flank of the Kananaskis Range.
Maps: Peter Lougheed Provincial Park Summer Trails brochure; 82 J/14.
Special attractions: Spectacular alpine scenery, Headwall Lakes, a small cascade, wildlife.
For more information: Park Superintendent, Peter Lougheed Provincial Park, Box 130, Kananaskis Village, Alberta, TOL 2HO. Ph: (403) 591-7222.
Finding the trailhead: From the Trans-Canada Highway, drive fifty kilometres south on Highway 40 to the junction with the Kananaskis Lakes Trail. Turn right and drive 2.5 kilometres and turn right again onto the Smith-Dorrien/Spray Road heading north. Continue north for twenty-five kilometres to the Chester Lake trailhead and parking lot. The trail begins on the old logging road heading east from the south end of the lot.

The hike: For years, the Headwall Lakes were rarely visited, with most hikers aiming instead for Chester Lake and its stock of cutthroat trout one drainage to the north. But today more people are setting off for the backcountry simply to see what lies over the next ridge. In the case of Headwall Creek, the answer is solitude, wildlife, and a pair of pewter lakes bound by bedrock and talus slopes.

Park at the southern end of the Chester Lake lot, near the access road. A system of old logging roads snakes south from the lot along the foot of the Kananaskis Range, and these old tracks have been designated as cross-country ski trails for winter use. The way to Headwall Lakes begins on the uppermost road, which is marked with a blue metal blaze.

Follow the blue markers for three kilometres as the road contours gradually southeast at the foot of Mount Chester. Shortly after the road cuts uphill, the blue markers fork left. Bear right here, now following yellow markers. The road drops down to Headwall Creek, fords the stream, and then clambers straight uphill to a ragged clearing well above the creek.

Look here for a trail leading north into the trees—an unmarked track worn into place by the common aim of dozens of hikers in recent years. The route eventually crosses a meadow and several stands of spruce before reaching timberline and a low headwall. Climb the headwall onto the limestone bedrock and bear left to the first lake. The first lake offers the most reasonable campsites, though you should pitch the tent at least 100 metres from shore. Stay on the righthand shore and follow the rock ramp to the left of the braided cascade to gain the second headwall and lake some 300 metres above. Total distance from the trailhead to the upper lake is seven kilometres.

The towering cliffs and peaks around the lakes are inspiration enough for many hikers, but some visitors may also thrill to a glimpse of bighorn sheep, mountain goats, or a grizzly bear. Elk and moose frequent the lower meadows and forest, and coyote tracks on the trail are not uncommon.

HIKE 71 *HEADWALL LAKES*

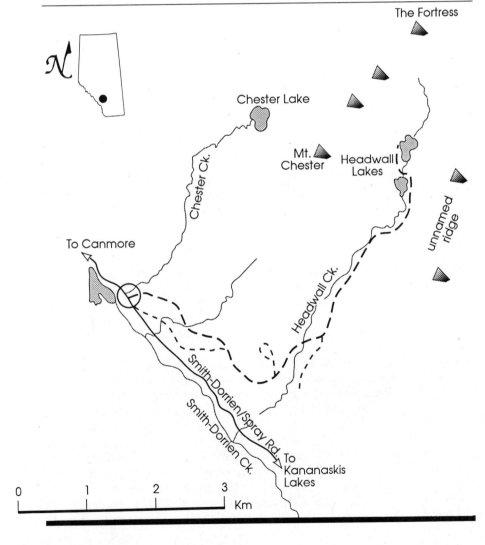

HIKE 72 *KING CREEK CANYON*

General description: An easy to moderate day hike through a rocky chasm at the base of the jagged Opal Mountains.
General location: East of Lower Kananaskis Lake in Peter Lougheed Provincial Park.
Maps: Peter Lougheed Provincial Park Summer Trails brochure; 82 J/11.
Special attractions: Outstanding scenery, King Creek Canyon, wildlife.

After spring runoff, King Creek Canyon provides ready access to the front of the Opal Range.

For more information: Park Superintendent, Peter Lougheed Provincial Park, Box 130, Kananaskis Village, Alberta, TOL 2HO. Ph: (403) 591-7222.
Finding the trailhead: The King Creek Canyon parking lot and trailhead is found on the east side of Highway 40 across from the intersection with the Kananaskis Lakes Trail (fifty kilometres south of the Trans-Canada Highway and just north of the winter closure gate on Highway 40). The trail begins as a self-guided interpretive walk on the south bank of the creek.

The hike: The King Creek interpretive trail provides hikers with direct access to the west front of the Opal Range, a spectacular line of grey peaks

HIKE 72 *KING CREEK CANYON*

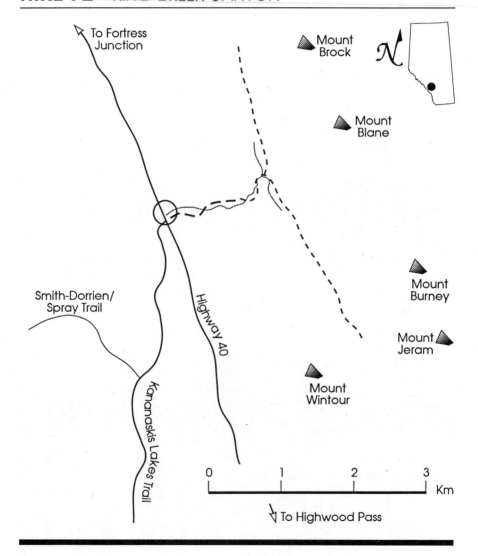

on the eastern boundary of Peter Lougheed Provincial Park. Log bridges cross the stream in the narrow canyon over the first kilometre, but the upper reaches can be negotiated only after seasonal runoff recedes, usually late July. At low water, hikers can rock-hop beyond the end of the official trail to the north and south forks of King Creek for a day of wandering among the high peaks. Your feet will probably get wet in the early going, so wear running shoes and carry an extra pair of socks.

The trail begins on the south bank of King Creek from the east end of the small parking lot. Numerous log bridges carry the trail directly up the stream channel, alternating from one wall of the canyon to the other. The interpretive trail ends about 800 metres above the mouth of the canyon. Continue along the stream bed for another kilometre, skipping from one boulder to the next and favouring the south bank for the easiest route. The creek bends north and east again before reaching the forks and the open slopes at the foot of Mount Blane.

Hikers can follow either fork, though the south fork climbs more gradually and eventually reaches a higher col than the north fork. Ford the stream and turn right along the east bank. There is no established trail, but the hiking is easy and the route straightforward. The Opal Range rises on the left, with Mount Burney and Mount Jerram as the most prominent peaks. On the right rises the knife edge of Mount Wintour. Watch for bear sign in the meadows (grizzlies sometimes ramble through this narrow corridor in search of ground squirrels and edible roots) and goats on the walls above.

Roughly four kilometres from the forks the grade climbs steeply to a 2,330-metre saddle between the southeast arm of Mount Wintour and the scooped face of Mount Jerram. Turn around and enjoy the view north along the rest of the Opal Range up to Mount Packenham. Retrace your steps to return to the trailhead, allowing about two hours for the six-kilometre hike out.

Wyndham-Carseland Provincial Park

HIKE 73 *JOHNSON'S ISLAND*

General description: An easy stroll along the banks of the Bow River.
General location: Sixty kilometres southeast of Calgary in Wyndham-Carseland Provincial Park.
Maps: Write for the park campground brochure.
Special attractions: The Bow River, trout fishing, bird watching.
For more information: Wyndham-Carseland Provincial Park, P.O. Box 100, Carseland, Alberta, TOJ OMO. Ph: (403) 934-3523.
Finding the trailhead: From Calgary, drive east on Highway 22X forty kilometres to Highway 24. Turn south on 24 and pass through the small town

of Carseland, continuing east and south on the main highway. Less than a kilometre after crossing the Bow River, turn right onto the park access road and drive to the day-use area at the end of the road. The trail begins along the river's bank.

The hike: When the highways west of Calgary are filled with hurrying weekenders, Wyndham-Carseland Provincial Park offers a pleasant getaway within an hour's drive on quiet roads *east* of the city. The park fronts

HIKE 73 *JOHNSON'S ISLAND*

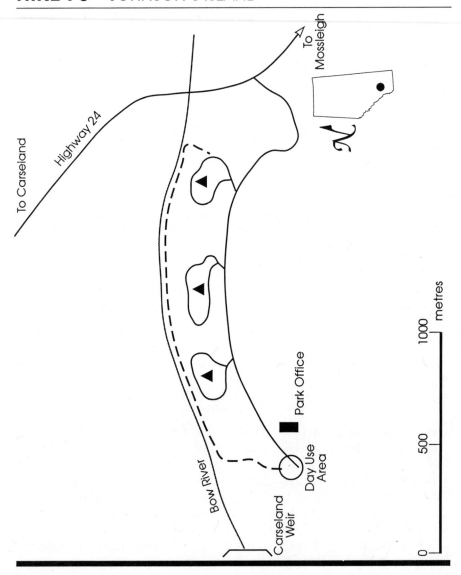

on the Bow River just downstream from the Carseland weir and trout fishing is the main attraction. Anglers use the two-kilometre Johnson's Island trail to fish the shoreline, but bird watchers also enjoy such ready access to the river. Highlights on the park's bird list include kingfisher, heron, double-crested cormorants, and white pelicans. The white pelican population is in decline throughout its range in North America, primarily because of insecticides entering the food chain. Hunters also take their toll, sometimes mistaking the pelican for snow geese.

Overnight campers at Wyndham-Carseland can reach the trail from any of the three campsite loops. Many campsites are within sight of the trail. Day-use visitors should follow the main park road to the picnic area and playground at the road's end, two kilometres from the entrance. The trail begins at a small information kiosk located between the parking lot and the river. The flat, graveled path parallels the river through thickets of alder and stands of cottonwood and poplar. Watch for white-tailed and mule deer, fox, and coyotes on the opposite bank, particularly at dawn and dusk. Return by the same route, or walk along the park road. In dry weather, the trail is adequate for wheelchair travel.

Fish Creek Provincial Park

HIKE 74 *FISH CREEK — EAST*

General description: An easy day hike along the bottomlands of the Bow River.
General location: South of downtown Calgary, within city limits.
Maps: Trail Map, Fish Creek Provincial Park.
Special attractions: Natural setting within the urban environment, waterfowl and songbirds, a variety of wildflowers and other riparian plants.
For more information: Fish Creek Provincial Park, Box 2780, Calgary, Alberta, T2P OY8. Ph: (403) 278-5640.

The hike: If you're not familiar with the fast-paced lifestyle favoured by Calgary's citizens, a day's visit to the city will leave you breathless. For longer stays, you'll want to know where Calgarians go to fill their lungs and relax. The answer is Fish Creek Provincial Park, an eighteen-kilometre greenbelt at the city's southern edge.

Highway 2, known as Macleod Trail within Calrgary's limits, bisects Fish Creek Provincial Park into two distinct halves. The west end follows Fish Creek from Shannon Terrace to Shaw's Meadow (see Fish Creek–West). The east end continues along Fish Creek from Glennfield to its confluence with the Bow River near the Bow Valley Ranch. From the confluence, park trails

181

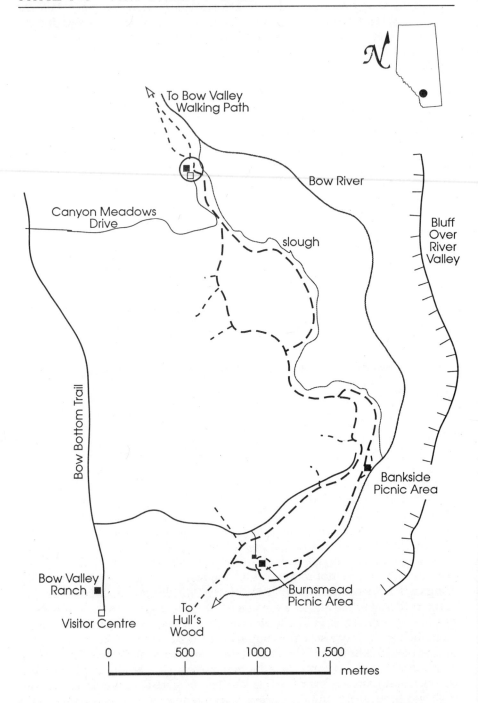

lead north along the Bow River to Mallard Point.

To reach the Mallard Point trailhead from Macleod Trail, turn east on Canyon Meadows Drive. Follow this winding road for roughly four kilometres, straight through the intersection with Bow Bottom Trail, to the cul de sac at Mallard Point. There are washrooms and benches next to the parking lot and a picnic area on the banks of the Bow River less than 100 metres to the northeast.

Two types of trails are found in the park. Paved routes are popular with bicyclists and roller skaters, but are wide enough for pedestrians to walk safely despite the occasional "traffic." You'll want to glance both ways before striding onto the pavement. More suited to hiking are the shale trails, which generally run closer to the rivers and creeks and pass through less developed terrain.

The hike from Mallard Point begins at the shale path at the head of the parking lot. This trail loops south for one kilometre along a side channel of the Bow River before connecting again with the paved trail system. Within another 500 metres, a second shale path drops away to the left of the paved trail. This trail follows the side channel down to the Bow River and then stays near the river bank for two kilometres to the Burnsmead picnic area. Watch for Canada and snow geese in the slough, herons fishing in the shallows, and deer on the opposite bank. Fox are sometimes seen on the slope of the bluff above the Bow River.

To complete the loop back to Mallard Point, take the Burnsmead access road up to the paved trail and turn right. This trail retraces your route by staying in the grassy meadows of the Bow River floodplain. The northern horizon offers glimpses of the downtown Calgary skyline.

HIKE 75   *FISH CREEK — WEST*

General description: A short, easy stroll along Fish Creek to an interpretive display overlooking an active heron rookery.

General location: Near the mid-point of Fish Creek Provincial Park at the southern edge of Calgary.

Maps: Fish Creek Provincial Park trail brochure.

Special attractions: Fish Creek, riparian plants and animals, a heron rookery.

For more information: Fish Creek Provincial Park, Box 2780, Calgary, Alberta, T2P OY8. Ph: (403) 278-5640.

Finding the trailhead: Fish Creek Provincial Park runs across the southern edge of Calgary's city limits. From Macleod Trail, drive 2.5 kilometres east on Canyon Meadows Drive to the intersection with Bow Bottom Trail. Turn south (right) and drive two kilometres on Bow Bottom Trail to the park entrance and the Bow Valley Ranch parking lot on the right. Park here and walk to the paved trail and visitor centre at the northwest corner of the parking lot.

The hike: Fish Creek Provincial Park is home to a surprising array of wildlife, from mule and white-tailed deer to black bear, cougar, and lynx. Moose, coyotes, foxes, and mink have also been sighted within park boundaries, and some 200 species of birds pass through or make their home here. One seasonal resident, the great blue heron, returns each year in large numbers to hatch and fledge its young along Fish Creek's banks.

The heron colony roosts from May through August of each year in the cottonwoods along Fish Creek just west of the Bow Valley Ranch Visitor Centre. A core area around the nesting sites is closed to visitor use, but hikers

HIKE 75   *FISH CREEK — WEST*

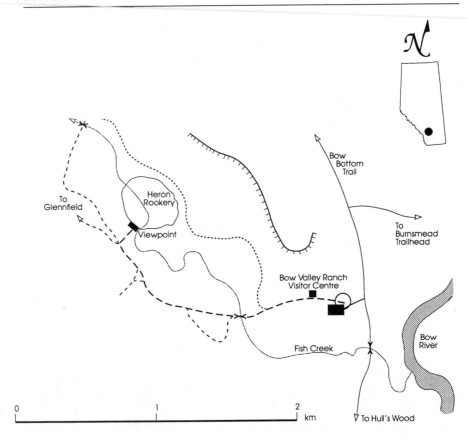

can still watch these magnificent birds from an overlook at Heron Flats. The overlook includes a large wooden deck with benches and an excellent interpretive display about the heron rookery.

From the Bow Valley Ranch Visitor Centre, walk west on the wide asphalt trail past the houses and outbuildings on the old ranch grounds. Bow Valley Ranch operated until the middle of this century, running cattle on the lush grasslands flanking Fish Creek and the Bow River. The trail soon crosses Fish Creek and enters an open, grassy meadow, intersecting with the Midnapore access trail about 1.5 kilometres from the Bow Valley Ranch. Hikers share the paved trails with cyclists and skaters, so keep an ear tuned for warning bells and avoid making sudden changes in direction. There's usually plenty of room for passing traffic, but pedestrians should be particularly alert at trail junctions.

Bear right through the intersection, and watch for a grassy track to the right 200 metres ahead. This side trail leads to the Heron Flats overlook, about 100 metres from the asphalt trail. Adult herons begin arriving in the park in May to build nests high in the cottonwoods lining Fish Creek. Most of the young are hatched by late June, but late July is perhaps the best time to observe the birds—the adults come and go on fishing missions, and the fledglings are highly active, stretching their wings and hopping up and down in the nests.

Ardent bird watchers can easily spend several hours at the overlook—take lunch, plenty of drinking water, a shade hat, and binoculars—and still have time for a five-kilometre loop hike back to the trailhead. A gravel path begins to the right where the Heron Flats spur trail meets the asphalt trail; follow this path through the open bottomlands for one kilometre to a junction with an access trail on the left. Go straight 100 metres to another junction and turn right on a shale path heading directly north. Walk about 600 metres to a bridge over Fish Creek and turn right again after crossing the bridge.

From here, the shale path winds along the north bank of the creek, in and out of the cool shade of cottonwood stands. Bird watchers will enjoy this stretch too for its red-winged blackbirds, swallows, belted kingfishers, and waterfowl. After one kilometre the trail veers away from the creek, skirts a small oxbow, and meets an access trail leading to the neighborhoods on the bluff above. Turn right and continue another two kilometres through grassy meadows and scattered cottonwoods sandwiched between the bluff and Fish Creek. The trail passes the heron rookery again and drops quickly down to the creek before rejoining the asphalt trail. Turn left onto the asphalt, just 300 metres from the Bow Valley Ranch area.

APPENDIX

Going Metric

The metric system is used throughout Canada—road signs are posted in kilometres, elevations given in metres, and temperatures reported in Celsius.

To convert metres into feet, multiply by 3.28. For example, Mount Assiniboine rises to 3,618 metres or 3,618 x 3.28 = 11,867 feet. Some Canadian maps were printed with elevations in feet. To convert feet into metres, multiply by 0.3048. Mount Rae is 10,560 feet or 10,560 x 0.3048 = 3,219 metres.

For quick conversions of kilometres into miles, figure every 10 kilometres equals 6 miles, thus 30 km = 18 miles, 80 km = 48 miles, and 90 km = 54 miles. These are rough estimates and are particularly useful when mentally converting traffic speed signs. For a more precise conversion, multiply the number of kilometres by 0.62. For example, 5 km x 0.62 = 3.1 miles; 90 km x 0.62 = 55.8 miles.

Bibliography

Alberta Wildlife Viewing Guide, Falcon Press, Helena, Montana, 1990, 112 pages.

Bear Attacks: Their Causes and Avoidance, Stephen Herrero, Hurtig Publishers, Edmonton, Alberta, 1985, 287 pages.

Canadian Rockies SuperGuide, Falcon Press, Helena, Montana, 1991, 368 pages.

The Canadian Rockies Trail Guide, Brian Patton and Bart Robinson, Summerthought Press, Banff, Alberta, 1990, 363 pages.

Handbook of the Canadian Rockies, Ben Gadd, Corax Press, Jasper, Alberta, 876 pages.

Kananaskis Country Trail Guide, Gillean Daffern, Rocky Mountain Books, Calgary, Alberta, 1985, 384 pages.

Plants of Waterton-Glacier National Parks, Richard J. Shaw and Danny On, Mountain Press Publishing, Missoula, Montana, 1979, 160 pages.

Waterton and Northern Glacier Trails for Hikers and Riders, Charles Russell, Beth Russell, John Russell, and Valerie Haig-Brown, Waterton Natural History Association, Waterton Park, Alberta, 1991, 110 pages.

Wildflowers of the Canadian Rockies, George Scotter, Hurtig Publishers, Edmonton, Alberta, 1986, 170 pages.

HIKING NOTES

HIKING NOTES

HIKING NOTES

HIKING NOTES

Out here–there's no one to ask directions

. . . except your **FALCON** GUIDE.

FALCONGUIDES is a series of recreation guidebooks designed to help you safely enjoy the great outdoors. Each title features up-to-date maps, photos, and detailed information on access, safety, side trips, and more. The 6 x 9" softcover format makes every book an ideal travel companion as you discover the scenic wonders around you.

FALCONGUIDES . . . leading the way!

Order today! Toll-free 1-800-582-2665
FREE catalog! No purchase necessary.

P.O. Box 1718, Helena, Montana 59624

FALCON GUIDES ★ *Starred titles are new in the* **FALCON** GUIDES *series.*

★ Angler's Guide to Alaska	$ 9.95
Angler's Guide to Montana	$ 9.95
Back Country Byways	$ 9.95
Beartooth Fishing Guide	$ 7.95
Floater's Guide to Colorado	$11.95
★ Floater's Guide to Missouri	$ 9.95
Floater's Guide to Montana	$ 8.95
★ Hiker's Guide to Alaska	$ 9.95
★ Hiker's Guide to Alberta	$ 9.95
Hiker's Guide to Arizona (revised)	$ 9.95
Hiker's Guide to California (revised)	$11.95
Hiker's Guide to Colorado (revised)	$11.95
Hiker's Guide to Hot Springs in the Pacific NW	$ 9.95
Hiker's Guide to Idaho (revised)	$11.95
Hiker's Guide to Montana (revised)	$ 9.95
Hiker's Guide to Montana's Continental Divide Trail	$ 9.95
Hiker's Guide to Nevada	$ 9.95
Hiker's Guide to New Mexico	$ 9.95
★ Hiker's Guide to Oregon	$ 9.95
★ Hiker's Guide to Texas	$ 9.95
Hiker's Guide to Utah (revised)	$11.95
★ Hiker's Guide to Virginia	$ 9.95
Hiker's Guide to Washington	$ 9.95
★ Hiker's Guide to Wyoming	$ 9.95
Hunter's Guide to Montana	$ 9.95
Recreation Guide to California National Forests	$ 9.95
Rockhound's Guide to Montana	$ 7.95
Scenic Byways	$ 9.95
★ Scenic Byways II	$ 9.95
★ Trail of the Great Bear	$12.95
★ Trail Guide to Glacier National Park	$ 9.95
★ Virginia Scenic Drives	$ 9.95

Falcon Press Publishing Co.–call toll-free 1-800-582-2665